MY RIVER of LIFE

MY RIVER
of LIFE

RON JONES

*'Life is like an uncharted river, we are never
certain what's around the bend.'*

HISTORY INTO PRINT

First published by
History Into Print, 56 Alcester Road,
Studley, Warwickshire B80 7LG in 2008
www.history-into-print.com

ISBN: 978-1-85858-322-8

A Cataloguing in Publication Record
for this title is available from the British Library.

Typeset in New Baskerville
Printed in Great Britain by
Cromwell Press Ltd.

CONTENTS

ACKNOWLEDGEMENTS

I thank my wife Joan for the kindness and patience she has always given to me, especially through my times of illness and worries. Without her support I could not have written this story.

I also extend my sincere thanks to our good friend Chris Chance for her skilful help in translating my writing and typing it into a decipherable order.

I offer my thanks also to Express Newspapers for their kind permission to use photographs previously used by themselves in the Story of the Battles of Normandy.

PREFACE

I dedicate this brief autobiography I have named "My River of Life" to the memories of my parents who, like thousands of others, suffered the hardships of the 1920s and early 1930s and were still haunted by the dreadful loss of life of the First World War, made worse by having to live in tiny back-street houses within the cities and having to survive by their own means with little or no help.

My father, as many like him, had to endure the trauma and horrendous experiences of trench warfare. He was a Lance-Corporal in the West Yorkshire Light Infantry, a regiment which had lost most of its men during the many battles of the First World War. He himself was wounded twice during those senseless battles of the Somme. Words like 'trauma' and 'battle fatigue' never seemed to be understood in those hard times, but I know he had suffered uncomplaining for most of his life and asked for very little.

My mother, between the ages of fourteen and sixteen, worked in a laundry for six days a week with a nine hour day. Her job was to repair any damage to the garments in the process of cleaning. When she left to do war work at the Austin Motor Company, she was given a letter of thanks from the Manager commending her on her loyalty and hard work, which must have helped and encouraged her during those hard days.

Some years after they were married, they eventually had five children, I being the fourth, so seven of us were living in a tiny back-street house in Birmingham. Their dedication to us was paramount in trying to bring us up properly under adverse conditions, and they instilled in us the need to behave decently and have respect for others. Mother had a saying, 'If you have nothing to laugh at, then laugh at yourself and your problems' which was helpful to us in later life and kept us a happy family.

I offer no apologies for their methods of survival which they achieved in those difficult times.

THE REASON I WROTE THIS STORY

I moved to Alvechurch some forty six years ago with my wife Joan and our children. A quiet village then but I had memories of it from childhood. The Worcester Canal runs through it and I remember the enjoyable days fishing here in the canal; it was a bus ride from Birmingham and the days out here I remember so well.

The village comprises many things today – a Women's Institute, a Village Hall where the locals can organise little shows or a Bring and Buy sale etc. There are three Pubs, a Cricket and Football Club, and a Sports and Social Club. The old St. Lawrence Church which stands on a hill overlooking the village has a fine Norman clock tower and there is also a small village green with a Dedication Stone in remembrance of those from the village who fought and died for their country.

There was no Ex-services Association in the village although quite a number of the residents were members of some kind of Military Association in other areas. Unknown to me and many others at the time, in early 2003 a group of ex-service men and women had conceived the idea of starting up an Alvechurch Association. There were a handful of men, Arthur Pearsall, Russ Moreton, Horace King and Fred Bradford, who first discussed the possibility of such an organisation. The idea was advertised in the local Village Magazine and soon other ex-service men and women became involved. A meeting was then held at the Alvechurch Social Club on the 11th June 2003. A committee was formed with Arthur Pearsall as Chairman, John Hoccom as Secretary and his wife Auriel as the Treasurer. The Alvechurch Ex-services Association was now formed.

It was some two years later when I joined the Association and it soon became apparent to me, the hard work and sincerity of the Committee and what it stood for, and for that I wanted to become more involved and help where I could. About two years later after chatting to John and Auriel about war experiences, Auriel remarked, "Ron, people like you should write stories of your experiences for your children." "But I'm hopeless at writing – it's my worst subject" I replied, "my writing is poor and my spelling isn't so good either!" Well, I knew she was right and I gave it some thought.

I was then eighty two years old and my memory was not so good, but I set about scribbling notes of what I could remember. I thought I should write those memories as a story and I felt I owed it to my parents for the manner in which they brought us all up under difficult circumstances, and for my wife Joan and our family.

Part of the story is dedicated to those Army friends who lost their lives during those dreadful days from Normandy to Bremen in Germany. Perhaps I may be forgiven in trying to show some funny incidents as well as the worrying and traumatic experiences which my Army colleagues and I had to face.

Ron Jones – 2008

CHAPTER ONE

I was born on the 10th February 1925 and christened Ronald. Probably the most important date in our lives is our birthday, a date we never forget and are constantly reminded of. But we know nothing until our brain starts to function some time later and most of us try to think about what we first remember. Someone once told me he remembered the day he was born – knowing nature, I suppose anything is possible. I was a bit of a slow starter in that respect, and later in life my eldest sister told me that my mother had remarked that she had less trouble with me than all the other children as I was always asleep, never crying, and all she had to do was to pop me in the pram when she had things to do and I was off to sleep, but I believe later in life I was to be her biggest worry.

My first introduction to life I remember, was falling backwards whilst I was strapped into a child's high chair which had fallen back against the wall, and I woke up yelling my head off. My mother came in from outside after hearing me bawling and sat me up again close to the wall and I promptly went back to sleep.

I was the fourth child to be born. There were two older sisters and a brother and two years later came my younger sister. So now there were seven of us including my mother and father living in a small back street house. To get to our house we had to go up an entry between two houses and immediately turn left into ours. This was known as a back-house which was joined to the one in the front. In the left hand corner of the back yard was a through house and the front room was used as a Greengrocer's shop. As many older people will remember, there were two communal toilets each side of the back yard, in which the remains of a daily paper hung, (never the Financial Times!). I'm sure no-one read them, understood them or needed them! On the right hand side was a much bigger house with a very large shed at the back, which as a child always puzzled me. I used to stand on a stool and look through the window watching an elderly man making large boxes. One day I asked my father why he was making these boxes. He replied, "They are not boxes, son, they are coffins. This is what he does for a living." The old chap had always lived in this large house all by himself, and I had no idea at that time that this house would eventually change our lives. I was not to realise as I was too young, that we were extremely poor financially and my father was unemployed and struggling to survive.

The back houses had a black cast iron grate and on the left of that was a black gas cooker and on the right was a large green painted food cupboard. Mother was always polishing that grate! Sometimes a man in a smart suit and carrying a brief case would walk into the house and ask my mother to open the cupboard and he would look inside. I found out some time later he was called the 'means test man.' He would examine the contents of the cupboard to see if we had enough food to go around, and if not we would be allowed two shilling and sixpence for extra food. The neighbours had rigged up a warning to notify each other when he was on his rounds. When we knew this, Dad would empty most of the food into a box and hide it in the cellar. However, what we lacked in money we were never short of love and kindness from our parents.

My parents were quite small – Mother was only 4ft 11ins. and Father 5ft 4ins. When I was about seven, I heard Dad talking to his friend about the First World War and he was getting rather upset. Mom always comforted him at these times as she was a marvel at that. I found out that he went into the Army at seventeen and was in the West Yorkshire Infantry as a Lance Corporal and at seventeen and a half he was in the Battle of the Somme and wounded twice. At my young age if anyone had told me about soldiers suffering from trauma I would not have know what it meant. I was not to know that one day this would have an effect on my own life in later years and how I would understand my father. Sometimes he would come in and be very upset and start swearing badly and would upset us all, but Mother knew how to handle the situation because she understood. It appeared that many ex-soldiers were in the same situation and if they stood on the street corner talking, a policeman would promptly move them on in case they might be inciting trouble – as if they had not had enough!

At the age of five I had to start going to school which was quite local to us, it was St. Thomas's in Bath Row about a quarter of a mile from home. Across the road from the school was St Thomas's Church with its fine steeple it stood out above everything around. The only times I went into it was when we had to go there for singing hymns or to see a slideshow on religious matters.

Myself, I had no desire to visit it for any reason even at that age I was very independent of my thoughts on religion.

During the early part of the war it was destroyed in a bombing raid in December 1940, but it left the steeple and front entrance still standing. Years later it was made into a peace hall by the council which I considered a fine thing to do.

About fifteen years ago I got interested in the remains of this church and I decided to paint three pictures of it in water colours. One I gave to my sister Pamela, one I still have myself and one I sold at a car boot sale for five quid, (but I was resigned to the fact I would never be rich many years earlier).

My mother was a good looking woman and always tried her best to look prim and smart. One day I heard my Dad's friend say, "George you are a lucky man to have a wife like that." "I know" he said, "she never stops working – but I may have some good news for her tomorrow." My father it appeared, had got himself a full time job working for the Birmingham Corporation Tramway Department. It was a turn for the better for my mother, but she continued to work hard for us all as we were still very young and were quite a handful in a small house and although my father was now bringing in an extra couple of pounds a week, it was still hard for Mom though it never stopped her from being kind. I remember a tramp coming up the yard one day, begging for food and she promptly gave him a large crust of bread and a lump of cheese out of the cupboard. My Dad was quite angry when he found out, "Giving away hard earned food" he said.

One day my parents let my two older sisters take me to a local park, Cannon Hill, but they did not keep their eyes on me enough and I was running all over the place. I spotted a girl on a swing going very high up and I thought it would be fun to run underneath when she was up at the top, but I did not run fast enough and was well and truly clobbered by the swing! I knew nothing until I came to in the Queen's

Hospital. I was covered in blood as it had split my head open. When I had been stitched up, my sisters carried me home to worried parents. Some months later I was in the same park with my brother Jim, and I was running across a cricket pitch when I was struck on the side of my head and was completely spark out with the force of the hard ball! I was fast becoming a source of worry to my parents though it was not to end there.

At that period of time the building of the Queen Elizabeth Hospital had started up the Bristol Road on old farm land. My father went to investigate and he took me with him. We found a stream still running where the old farmer had planted water cress. We went every Sunday, or at least he did, and he brought back bags of this water cress and sold it to the neighbours for a penny a bunch, which helped the income. Once I went with him and noticed a small pond with things in which had four legs. "They are newts" my Dad told me. The following week I asked him if I could have some, so he acquired a large sweet jar for me which I filled with newts with the aid of a net, then started to sell these to the local kids for a penny each, as they had never seen any before. One day my father told me off as I had left two of them in the jar and forgotten them. "You must never leave them in the jar with such little water – they need lots of clean water" he said. Well, on each side of the yard was a wash house with a large copper boiler which was shared by the neighbours, so on Sunday morning I put these two newts in the boiler in fresh cold water and then again forgot all about them, After coming home from school on Monday, I went to put some fresh water in the large jar so I could transfer the newts, but the lady who lived in the front house which backed on to ours, was in the wash house doing her washing. When I asked her what she had done with the two newts, she seemed rather annoyed and went straight to my mother. "I've been wondering what the hell's been mucking up my bloody washing" she said, "your Ronny's left newts in the boiler and I've had slimy stuff all over the sheets and pillow cases I put in!" We were not in favour at all, as only a few weeks before Dad was putting up a narrow shelf in the pantry which backed onto hers and he used some very large nails which he had acquired to support the wood, and one nail went straight through the single brick wall and smashed one of her jars of pickles. But it soon got forgotten as we were really all very friendly – most of the time!

4

Although things seemed to change day by day, we were still obviously very poor. My father, now working in Birmingham city, had found out that the Daily Mail Newspaper Company had somehow set up a form of charity for the poor, and would supply boots, shoes, socks and pullovers to those in real need. Although the socks and pullovers were real wool, they were easily recognised by the colour which was a dark navy blue.

One Saturday my Dad took my brother and me into town and applied for these items. We were both given a pair of boots, a pair of socks and a pullover. I think I was about seven at that time. A couple of weeks later, at school, we had a gym lesson but the hall we had to use had a polished wooden floor, so it was necessary to take off our boots. The problem was, the boots had to be placed in the corner and half of them were the Daily Mail boots, so it was a bit of a scramble to sort them out after the lesson. When I went home I knew I had the wrong boots on, and when my mother saw them she looked at me and said, "What have you done? Those are not your boots, they are miles too big." With a frustrated look, she grabbed my hand. "Come with me" she ordered, and quickly marched me back to the school. As we went up the main street, she spotted a woman with her son who was walking in his blue socks and carrying a pair of boots in his hand. As he was taller than me, it was obvious he had my boots and could not get them on! After a quick discussion between my Mom and his, we did an exchange there and then in the street.

There was always something happening to cause my mother worry. It was quite a thing in the mornings for her to get her five children off to school. Both my brother and I wore braces to hold up our trousers, and one morning the only button on the back of my brother's trousers came off just as we were about to go out. So my mother, in her usual hurried way, quickly sewed the button back on. Later, when he came home he was a bit upset. Evidently he'd needed to go to the toilet while he was at school but could not get his trousers off as Mom had accidentally sewn the button to his shirt as well! So after pulling the button off again, he had to tie the braces around his waist to hold up his trousers!

We often talked about these incidents in later life and it was always a source of amusement – but I felt quite sorry for my older sister,

Pamela, at one time. My father always repaired our shoes, as many fathers did in those days – usually on the kitchen table. However, my sister's shoes had been patched up so many times there was very little Dad could do; so he decided to take her down to the town and try to get some Daily Mail shoes for her. When they returned home, my sister was wearing boys' boots and was crying her eyes out. It appeared that there were no more girls' shoes left but Dad had insisted she could not walk back as she was, so they gave her the boys' boots. For the next three days she had to go to school in those boots and each morning cried not to have to wear them, but Mom had always insisted we should not miss school for anything. However, in the meantime my Dad did a deal with his friend down the street and did some sort of swap and got my sister some shoes. She was then quite happy and things all turned out O.K.

At that very early age I knew nothing about real life, as I never ventured far from home only when my mother occasionally took me to see her sister, my aunt, who lived only a short tram ride away. I knew nothing then of what was in store for me, and how eventually we all had to slot into life and go along with the tide as we grew up.

CHAPTER TWO

Now came a bend in that river of life which was about to change our lives for the better. It was late 1936 and I was coming up to twelve years old, my eldest sister was seventeen and my other older sister was fifteen and both had jobs. We were all growing up in this tiny house making it very difficult for our parents. My mother was a very bright person and would always like to settle down to read a book after her hard days work. She started to do a competition in the Sunday Mercury paper; it was called the 'Eights' – eight letters were given and you had to find a series of words from them. Within five weeks, Mom had won the equivalent of about ten weeks of my father's wages! We all ended up with new clothes; coats, shoes, trousers and hats for my brother and me and dresses etc for my sisters. We also had a battery driven wireless which Mom used to sit up and listen to in the evenings.

The only real problem now was the smallness of the house and there was very little room for comfort. My three sisters had to sleep in the same bed and my brother and I shared in the attic. Unknown to us a change was to come very suddenly.

One Saturday mid-day the elderly man who lived in the large corner house and made the coffins, came in to talk to my parents. We had always been on good terms with him and in the past he had helped us out when things had been broken. I heard Mom saying 'yes' to everything he said and seemed very pleased. When he went she shrieked with joy! He had come to tell us that he had retired and was leaving and had suggested that he would have a word with the Landlord, as he considered we should have his house. A few days later we heard that we could have the house although at an increased rent, but nothing was going to stop us. By the end of the week we were in!

All the things we owned were in after about two hours as we didn't have a lot to start with.

The house was so different to the one we had been living in. It consisted of a large living room, a hallway leading to a front door that took us straight out into the street, a front room which was hardly ever used, a kitchen and a large pantry. The old man had left a very large six-legged table which we believed he had used for assembling the coffins. This was scrubbed spotlessly clean and was now our dining table which was covered with a beautiful green table cloth with tassels all around which our parents had bought from the local pawn shop. By the end of the week, with the aid of everyone, the house had been thoroughly cleaned including the four bedrooms, to the delight of us all.

The following weekend our parents had a house warming party with all our friends and during this very happy party my mother, with a glass of stout in her hand said, "I name this house 'The Happy House'" and it was, even many years later. When she was ninety one years old, living in a flat by herself she regularly reminded us of the parties we had in the 'Happy House.' But it was she who made it like that. She had a saying, 'if you have nothing to laugh at then laugh at yourself and the things that have happened to you.'

Most of my time was spent in the large work shed out the back which had belonged to the old chap but was now ours. I learned so much and found I was very handy and practical using the tools in there. This practical way I had developed was to hold me in good stead in years to come, especially from an engineering point of view. But there was one thing I was bad at and that was writing. I could never write neatly or fluently when I was young. I remember my school teacher when one day he was checking our compositions. We were all sitting silently listening to the results and he suddenly shouted out, "Jones, I can't understand you – your drawings are fine and your general art work is good, but your writing looks as if a cat has dipped his tail in the inkwell and dragged it over the paper!" which started all the kids giggling. I had very little interest in writing and I now wonder how I started writing this story and how, or if, I will finish it.

I was still not quite twelve and very small in height and always maintained a young appearance. Most people thought I was much younger than my real age but I was very agile and I became a member of the child athletic team at school and we gave physical fitness demonstrations at Bingley Hall in Broad Street, Birmingham but my height was the biggest handicap especially when vaulting.

Across the street from our house was a shop that sold everything and it was run by a Mr. and Mrs. Simpson who had a son named Kenny who I tagged along with for some time. He was twelve months older than me and very much taller. His father ran a small band and had two cars in the garage at the side of the shop. In comparison with all the neighbours in the street, they were classed as very rich, as no-one else around owned cars. Very often his parents went out on Saturday nights and they would ask my parents if I could stop with their son while they were out, but I found him a spoilt kid who had everything he asked for. One Saturday he showed me his marvellous Hornby train set which was permanently set up, and all his other toys and things that I could never dream of owning, and he would often help himself to anything out of the shop. On another Saturday night he was rather excited and wanted me to see what his mother had bought. He said that it sucked the dirt up off the floor and was called a vacuum cleaner – I had never even heard of one. He insisted that I should see it work, so he plugged it into the supply. "Watch this" he said. Hanging on a line by the fire were some silk stockings his mother had put there to dry and he sucked every one into the vacuum! "Don't tell my Mom" he said, "I can get some more out of the shop." When my Dad found out he said, "I always thought that bloody kid was nuts!"

Kenny's mother regularly gave us tuppence each on Saturdays so we could go to the Broadway Cinema in Bristol Street, to watch the Cowboy films. The poor old doorman had no chance of controlling all these kids waiting to get in when the doors opened at two o'clock. When it did open he was flattened against the wall as they surged past. But lots of kids got in without paying as the first ones in would run to the front of the cinema and open the fire doors to let their mates in, then the attendant would try and drag them out again! One particular week there was a film called "The Lives of the Bengal Lancers" and all the kids screamed as the Lancers wielded their spears and swords. Being an old cinema there were small gas lights on the walls which were always left on. At the interval some of the youngsters would climb up the walls to light their cigarettes on them, and the attendant would go round telling them off – but it was a tough area and the kids never took any notice!

That same Saturday night I reluctantly went again to stay at the shop with Kenny. After a while he disappeared somewhere and I sat quietly by the fire reading a comic. Suddenly he appeared from upstairs; he had a sheet wrapped around him and was wielding a long thin knife, (the one his mother sliced the ham with in the shop). He shouted, "Look, Bengal Lancers!" then came over to me and thrust the knife into the comic and straight through into my leg. When he realised what he had done, he raided the shop for sticking plasters and plastered up my leg, all the time saying how sorry he was. The following day there was a bit of a row over at the shop. "Your Kenny's bloody barmy!" my Dad said to his Dad. "Yes I know" was the reply.

A few weeks later I stayed there again all Saturday afternoon and we sat there bored, looking at his toys. Then he had a brainwave as what to do. "Let me show you my Dad's other car" he said. Now that was more interesting to me as I always wanted to know how cars worked. "I'll show you how they work" he said. What he did not know was that at home I had a manual on a 1929 Austin 12hp with all the diagrams of the engine, gearbox, transmission etc. These things fascinated me and I soon learned how cars worked; I even knew the firing order of the engine and how the crankshaft moved the pistons in the correct order. There was very little I did not know about a basic petrol driven car but I had never sat in one. "Come on" said Kenny, "let's start it up, it's easy." Well I was not happy about this at all, knowing what he got up to. However we sat in the car but I couldn't see over the front panel and I told him this.

"You shouldn't be such a short-arse" he replied, and promptly switched on the engine. My legs were too short to reach the pedals, but at the back of the steering wheel was a hand throttle which he did not know about. I kept lifting this lever and revving the engine. He got very angry when I told him how it was connected to the carburettor. "You don't know that" he said, and when I told him what I knew about the engine he was very sharp and told me to "sod off home!" He opened the gate then slammed the door.

After about three weeks, my mother noticed I had stopped going over to the shop. "What's wrong" she asked, "what's happened? It's not like you to stop going to see Kenny." I told her what he had said and why, and she was horrified that I had been in the car with the engine running, and she gave me a right telling off. I had to promise that I would not get in it again. The thing about my parents was that they never did wallop me or any of the other four children, but I know that other kids around were walloped by their parents for less.

One day as I was coming out of school, I met Kenny and he said, "Why haven't you been over to see me?" "Because you told me to sod off" I replied. "No I didn't" he said. "Yes you bloody well did" I said angrily. "O.K. I apologise – come over on Saturday and help me make the plank motor I've started on." Reluctantly I agreed as in these areas very few kids had things like scooters or bikes and a craze was going around building what we called plank motors. To make these you had to acquire a plank of wood about five feet long and about eight inches wide, then scavenge an old discarded pushchair or pram and using the pair of smallest wheels, attach a piece of wood about four inches wide to the axle, put a hole in the middle of this wood and also in the front end of the plank, then bolt them together and this was the front steering. The larger wheels would be bolted in the same way to the rear of the plank. If there was a seat in the pram or pushchair this would be used as your seat. The front axle would be controlled with a piece of rope nailed to each side of the axle and all you needed then was someone to push you along to a spot with a downward slope. Once on the way the pusher would jump on the back as well. (In our case it was usually me as he liked to give the orders!)

Ours was finally completed but not without arguments. We argued about who got the most parts for it, who did the most work and who had the best ideas. "Shall we try it out next Saturday?" asked Kenny. "O.K." I agreed. "I know a nice quiet spot to go to" he said. Like other kids who had them, we needed a quiet road with little traffic. We found it worked quite well but the only problem was that Kenny had to stop it by pressing his feet on the front wheels! After about half a dozen goes I complained that it was about time I had a go on the front and he could push it for a change. He reluctantly agreed, saying, "Your turn tomorrow, but we'll find a longer hill." When we came home from school the following day we towed the plank motor to the top of a hill called Holloway Head. At the top was the school we both went to and it was a long downward slope to Bristol Street. He said, "Jump on and keep out of the middle of the road." As he was much bigger and stronger than me he really gave me a hefty push and within seconds he jumped on the back, balling out instructions to me. But the road was much smoother than the others and we soon gathered speed.

After a short while he shouted, "Put your feet on the wheels, we're going too fast!" but as my shoes were a bit loose on me the one shoe flipped off and no way could I stop it. As he was continually shouting at me I lost concentration and I had not noticed a double-decker corporation bus which had stopped to pick up passengers. Within seconds we had slammed straight into the back of it. The front wheels went under the back of the bus and I was wedged with my face flat against the rear end! The conductor got off the bus, telling us off as he dragged us free. The front wheels were ruined and I had lost my shoe. My friend was very angry with me. "You stupid prat!" he shouted, and as I was pretty shaken up and didn't like what he said, I lashed out at him as hard as I could but he grabbed both my wrists to stop me. After that tussle, the bus conductor hauled us onto the pavement and gave us a good telling off. We never spoke all the way home, and my legs hurt as they were covered in scratches from going under the bus. He walked on one side of the road towing his blessed plank motor, while I walked on the other side. I had no intention of telling my mother or father, and luckily there was no-one in when I got home so I lay on the settee and fell fast asleep hoping they would never find out!

It was now June 1937. I'd had my twelfth birthday in February and things seemed to be going all right. I believe that life is like a river – it starts out as a very small trickle of a stream and it flows around bends, not knowing what's around the corner. It gets bigger and stronger and at each bend things are different, sometimes going straight and smooth and placid – but there is always another bend to face. I was feeling very contented as I had good parents and we were still happy in our house, having parties for various occasions and our friends loved coming round especially when Dad sang his army songs, some of them very funny.

"Don't you think you should find a job now?" my mother said one day. I was nearly twelve and a half now and most boys had part-time jobs at that age. "There's a job going at the grocers on the corner" said Mom, "I will have a word with them tomorrow. It's just delivering parcels on Saturdays." She then arranged for me to see the man who ran the shop. It appeared that they had a three-wheeled basket/carriage which would be filled with parcels of groceries and I would have to deliver them to people who couldn't get to the shop – sometimes it might be two loads. At three shillings and sixpence per week I accepted the job. I worked there until I was fourteen years old, when I left school. All that time I never had a tip or a raise, but I never missed a delivery. When I left, the grocer gave me a box of biscuits and that was that! I had no plans for a full time job as everyone left school at that age.

A couple of years previously, my mother acquired an old treadle sewing machine so that she could do jobs to make a bit of extra cash. When she had left school she worked in a laundry, not to do washing but to repair damaged clothing and sew buttons back on that had been pulled off by the machines. She was seventeen years old when she left and they gave her a certificate saying what a good worker she was and she was very proud of it. So she was capable of making a few quid doing repairs for the locals. My father had other ideas; he now worked in the tram department yard and sometimes a tram or bus would be brought in that had seen the last of its days, and would be dismantled. In these vehicles the seats were covered in quality leather. My Dad would remove some of this leather as it was still in good condition and he would get five or six pieces, wrap them around his body, tie it with string then put his overalls back on and come home with them. My mother, although she objected, would make shopping bags out of these pieces of leather using her old machine and sell them for a shilling each. When I was working at the grocers I would see women come into the shop carrying these bags – I think half the street seemed to have them and they lasted for ever.

One day I saw my Dad coming up the hill – he always came home that way on a Saturday lunch time when he had finished work. He appeared to be limping badly and his leg seemed stiff. I ran into the house calling, "Mom, Dad's hurt himself, he's limping up the hill."

Mom looked a bit puzzled, and when he came in he went straight into the work shed, undid his belt and from down his leg he produced a long roll of white material. Written on the material were bus numbers and destination place names. These were indicators that went on the front of the bus and the conductors altered by turning them with a handle when the bus went on a different route. "What am I supposed to do with that?" asked Mom. "I thought you could boil it in the wash house and get the letters off, then make curtains or skirts for the girls" he replied. And that's exactly what she did!

Whatever Dad did it was never for himself, always for us. Although he was not very big he was a tough old devil and always stood up for himself and wanted us to be the same. One day he got hold of some boxing gloves and encouraged my brother and me to a bit of boxing at times. My brother was slightly built but was very agile and fast. We would start boxing but after a while we would lose our tempers and start scrapping properly. When that happened, Dad would stop us and make us shake hands.

As in all places like ours, there was always the local bully who, one Saturday, was provoking a friend of ours to fight. "Leave him alone" I shouted. At that the bully came after me as he always seemed to go after someone smaller than himself. He chased after me and I was a bit scared of him so ran up our entry and into our back yard. My Dad was feeding his chickens (he had a small run and pen for them). When he saw me running away he shouted, "Stop, stand up to him" and at that I had no choice. Even though my Dad was there, this kid came up to me and started to wallop me. "Come on, hit him back" shouted my Dad, so I had to. Eventually the bully ran off but I know I had the worst end of the stick though I know I gave him some as well. My Dad said, "You will find that a bully will back off when someone stands up to him." All this sounded very hard to me but it taught me a lot for later years.

I was thirteen years old now and I was getting reminded that I was not far off from leaving school. I was regularly asked what I wanted to do but I could never seem to make up my mind. My brother had turned fifteen and was already working in a factory on a production line. He was small and slightly built – the word 'obese' hardly existed in those days as people seemed to work much harder physically then, and most people walked to work and back home again. The main transport was either bicycle or tram. Even getting to hospital could be a problem. I seem to remember that about four times I was carried to the Accident Hospital. The man living on the opposite corner of our yard was a trader and sold vegetables. He had to collect these goods on his handcart from a supplier at the bottom of Birmingham Bull Ring, a good mile away. One day he was helping his friend from the other side of the street, to repair his pigeon loft and he fell off the roof and broke his leg. He was put on his handcart and taken to the Accident Hospital about half a mile away. All this active way of life kept your weight down – to see a fat person was a very rare sight.

It was now 1939 and at fourteen years old I was expected to find a place of employment but I was still not sure what to do. There was no problem in getting a job in Birmingham as in practically every street there was some sort of factory especially in engineering. After all, Birmingham had earned the title as the workshop of the world. Every imaginable thing would be made here, there was practically nothing that could not be made. If we had had a big river running through the city we would have made ships! Most of the smaller factories, if they wanted workers would simply put a notice on the gate of the property asking for the type of people they wanted.

CHAPTER THREE

About two weeks after I had finished school, my Dad came home one evening from work and told me he had seen a notice outside a local factory asking for a youth for the tool-making trade and this seemed to appeal to me. The following Monday, after my mother had done her chores and I'd seen all the family go off to work with packed lunches etc, except my youngest sister who had to go to school, Mom said to me, "Come on, polish your shoes and comb your hair, I'm taking you to that factory to see if you can have that job." It was all bewildering and strange to me but I knew I had to go as it was all part of life and growing up. When we got to the factory the notice was still up and the sign said we had to go to the office upstairs. We went up the wooden stairs where everything seemed to be painted green. At the top of the stairs was a small room, again all painted green, and we saw a little wooden door about two feet square with a bell to press for attention. "Smarten yourself up" Mom said, and she pressed the bell. After about five minutes the little hatch door opened and a man in a brown overall looked at my mother. "I've brought my son to see about the job" she said. He immediately leaned through the hatch and said, "Oh he's very small isn't he?" Well I'd heard this remark so many times that I said smartly, "It doesn't mean I don't have any brains." "Don't be so cheeky" my mother said to me. The man just smiled and started to ask Mom questions. Within a few minutes he said to me, "Alright, you can start on Monday at eight o'clock – come into the factory through the main entrance." He gave me another smile and then we were on our way home, my mother continually telling me to be polite to the man.

On arrival at the factory I was met by the same man who had interviewed me and he said he was the shop floor manager. "The first thing I will do," he said, "is show you around the factory and what we do, then you will know your way around and where to go." I was rather surprised as it was all much larger than I had expected, but very interesting. The offices were above the main gate and on the right through this gate was a heat-treatment plant. "This is where we heat-treat all the tools after they are made which makes them strong and last longer" he told me. The next building on the right held the power supply which drove all the machinery in the factory. This was fascinating to me as it was a huge steam engine and the fly-wheel was about ten feet in diameter with a long heavy leather belt about ten inches wide being driven round the wheel, then the belt crossed the yard into the main department where it connected up to the main shaft which was driving all the machinery. "I thought you would like that" he remarked, "everyone seems to be fascinated by it." At the rear of that building was a drop-forging department with large hammer-like presses. "You will be working in the production department for about three months first," the manager said, "in this way you will become acclimatised to all the tools we use, like dies and jigs, and will get to know everyone then we will slowly get you into making these tools."

Things were going well but I was anxious to get out of the production shop although I was learning quite a lot. Then I started to spend some time in what was called the top shop, and in this place were quite a few older people doing hand work like polishing dies and getting them ready for the drop-forging shop. This is what really started to get me interested, but as a young boy the atmosphere seemed to get to me sometimes, the heat of the factory and the fumes etc. I was always glad to get fresh air down my lungs when I went home – but I got used to it after a while.

It was now coming up to the latter part of 1939 and there were reports in the newspapers of pending trouble on the continent and of Germany building up a massive military force and ignoring what was known as the Versailles Treaty. This was a treaty agreed in 1919 by all the countries involved or affected by the First World War, not to re-arm or threaten the neighbouring countries.

However, suddenly without warning, German attacked and invaded Poland. Great Britain stood alone in warning Germany to remove their troops from Poland or we would declare war on them and our

Government gave them until September 3rd to comply. On that Sunday morning probably everyone was listening to their radios hoping to hear that we could avoid the war. At eleven o'clock on that fateful day, our family was listening to the report and the bad news was given by Mr. Neville Chamberlain that we were at war with Germany. My eldest sister was engaged to an Army Sergeant and she and my mother cried with sorrow as Mom had experienced it all before. My father stood silent – he had been all through the last war. Myself, I hadn't had the experience and didn't understand the true consequence of it all. The whole country was stunned at what had happened; after all we had not yet fully recovered from the First World War. After it had been accepted that we were now at war, there were lots of talk and rumours etc – people tried to guess how long it would last, some thinking it may only last twelve months.

A British Expeditionary Force was sent to France, knowing now that Germany would not stop advancing into France. All or at least most of the factories were changing over to war work – munitions etc. Factories were being geared up to work harder and longer hours. It was illegal for a person of my age to work seven days a week but a lot of us did without being forced to do it.

But I must stop and think and realise that this story is about me and my family and how I might or might not react to any situation that I may be confronted with. I did not have any worries in that respect – after all I was brought up in a hard life and had to endure many hardships as all our family had, and if we could get a laugh out of life we would, even though things may not turn out as we might want or expect them to.

By now the Government was encouraging the Local Councils to organise evacuation of the young children to safer places out of the cities. The residents of small villages and towns were being asked to help and take in children from the larger towns and cities. Thousands of children were evacuated in this way and transported by rail and road to safer areas.

My young sister, Betty, was given that chance, but it did not work out well at all for her. She was first sent out to a rural area to our Aunt's house, but our Aunt, never having had children around before, did not understand children's needs or care, so after six weeks Betty came home. She was then sent to Ashby de la Zouch to a family prepared to look after her, but she was continually unhappy about her care there and was finally brought back by our mother who found Betty dirty and covered in fleas. Lots of children had unhappy experiences like this, but overall most of them had been treated with care and kindness and some lives had been saved by this scheme.

The war was not going very well for Britain and we were getting bombed by the Germans, which was considered to be inhumane killing of innocent women and children. People were getting very tired and strained with lack of sleep and having to spend long hours in air-raid shelters or trying to protect themselves in the cellars of their own homes. Our armies were being pushed back towards the beaches of Dunkirk. Gloom seemed to be settling in. I was now fifteen years old and as I was small and slightly built I was beginning to feel strained myself, not realising why. I was trying to take everything in my stride, working seven days a week, losing lots of sleep because of the raids, and not getting the right sort of food as it was all on ration – although my mother was doing her very best for all of us with what was available. I had heard the word 'vitamins' mentioned for the first time, and it appeared that the lack of these may have been the problem for everyone. But there was something else bothering me. I believed that hardship and hard work was not the problem – I could cope with that. I had now turned fifteen and a half and was feeling quite ill at times.

One night I had witnessed an elderly woman standing by her bedroom window with her house on fire, after it had been bombed. She had obviously received burns and was shouting for help. A.R.P. (Air Raid Precautions) men were trying to rescue her. This really upset me to see a woman in so much fear. I had two friends, brothers, whose father seemed to let them fend for themselves. They had to get all their own food to eat. "Where's your mother?" I asked them one night as we sat in an air raid shelter. "She's in the hospital – she has cancer" they said. After the raid was over, we brought them back home with us and Mom gave them some hot cocoa then I walked back to their house with them. "We're going to the hospital tomorrow, would you like to come and see our Mom?" they asked. I felt I could not refuse. When we got there, their mother was lying in the bed looking very pale and old. I stood by the door while the boys kissed her. She waved to me and I waved back but once again I felt deeply upset by this. Some weeks later I asked the boys how their mother was. "Oh, she is at home – she is on top of the sideboard in her coffin" they replied, "come home with us and see her." Very reluctantly I did and when we arrived there was no sign of their father. "Here she is" said the older boy, "come and have a look." At that he lifted the coffin lid and I saw this poor dead woman. I immediately felt very frightened and went straight home. All this was too much for me. I would get too emotional over these things; a bad thing for me if I was to face the world as a grown up man. But one thing I felt sure about was that these two kids had it tougher than me in their very early days, because of a neglectful father.

I was now understanding the real hardships of war and all the sorrowful things it brought. The wife of my father's best friend, who he had known in the First World War and had been in the same regiment, had died from cancer just before the Second World War had begun. His two grown up sons joined the Army as soon as the war had started but they were both killed at Dunkirk. My father came home one night and told my Mom that his friend had taken his own life in a horrendous way as he could not cope with the terrible news. My Dad was very upset but bad news like this was commonplace throughout wars.

There were also reports in the local newspaper of many sad things happening. We read one night of a young father who lived not far away, who had taken his wife and two small children into the air raid shelter at the bottom of his garden. During the air raid he went up into his house by himself to make his family a hot drink and while he was in the house a bomb dropped directly on the shelter killing his wife and children. Some time later he also took his own life as he felt responsible for their deaths by leaving them in the shelter. Many stories like this were heard and it was taking its toll on people who were in the bombing areas.

I was nearly sixteen and my father decided to take me to see the doctor as I was not feeling well. After quite a lot of talking the doctor told my Dad that for my age I was working too many hours without a break and losing so much sleep because of the raids coupled with the fact that the good food we needed was rationed. It was suggested that I take two weeks off work then work a normal week, i.e. forty eight hours, and I was given some sort of booster medicine. The following night my father came home with a dozen oranges – something I hadn't seen for a long time! We never asked our father where he got things from and he wouldn't tell us anyway. I started to feel better as soon as I had time off from work and kept to the forty eight hours a week after that. During this time my Dad had built a better chicken run up in the corner of the yard and acquired some more young chickens which he reared for food and fresh eggs, which gave us all a boost.

CHAPTER FOUR

About this time I felt I had to do something for myself. I was an impatient person and needed to control this. First I joined the Birmingham Athletic Institution in Severn Street, run by a Mr. James Hipkiss who taught 'Ju-jitsu' and 'Catchers Can' wrestling. Apart from keeping fit I found that this was just what I needed. (After the war Mr. Hipkiss became a therapist at the Orthopaedic Hospital in Northfield and became very well known). As I had cut down on my working hours I still thought I should be doing more so joined the Home Guard at Five Ways in Birmingham. At my first visit I was met by a big man by the name of Sergeant-Major Harcourt; but my old problem was still with me – he did not believe me when I told him I had just turned sixteen years old! "You look a bit young for sixteen" he said, "as well as being a bit on the short side!" but after I had convinced him that I was old enough to join, he said, "We will have a problem getting you a uniform but we will do our best." He tapped me on the head, "see you at nine o'clock on Sunday morning and I will introduce you to the rest of the Platoon." I walked off and felt very pleased I had been accepted.

It seemed to me that now was a good time to take stock of myself, as I felt I was on a straighter course of my River of Life. My mother was still providing little house parties for birthdays and such like, which always ended up with Dad singing his favourite Army songs – some of which were so funny, songs I had never heard before and never since, and Mom still referred to our home as the 'Happy House.' I now believed that I had almost identified myself, and better for knowing. I had accepted that I was never going to be very tall. I knew I could get very emotional over other peoples' sorrow. I was impatient. I was very practical in most things. I did not have a good education. I would always listen to peoples' views but had independent thoughts about everything. I was not religious. The school I had attended was an Elementary school and classed itself as Church of England and taught Christianity. Most religious things I just pushed aside. I believe that most religions started many years ago, and were off-shoots of certain cults that began in the dark ages and all these were born out of ignorance. There are many things in the Bible I believe are true, although somewhat distorted by religion. Some religions have developed over many years to be very powerful and peoples' belief is so strong that they are prepared to die and kill others for it. I think that this comes from brainwashing by their ignorant and misguided forefathers. That is what I believe and what has guided me through life.

After I had been in the Home Guard for a couple of months I settled in well and seemed to be accepted as one of the group. Our Platoon Commander was a Lieutenant Wilson who owned a book shop in Broad Street. He said one Sunday morning, "Sergeant-Major we must get Jones a uniform – we cannot have him being the only one on parade without one." "I will get something organised, Sir" he replied. This is going to be funny, I thought, as I was only five feet two inches at that time. Sergeant-Major Harcourt then detailed another sergeant to get the smallest uniform out of the stores and take me, with this uniform, to a tailor in Hurst Street by the Birmingham Hippodrome Theatre, to see what he could do for me. This tailor was called Harry Cohen and he was very well known by all the people and performers at the Hippodrome, for his speed and skill in altering clothes to be ready for the actors to go on stage.

Sergeant Brooks and I arrived at Harry's shop early on a Saturday morning. It was an old converted back street house similar to the one I was born in, with the old black fire grate and a set of stairs leading up the bedrooms. Everything seemed untidy – clothes all over the place as though he had no time to tidy it up. There was an old treadle sewing machine in the corner and it looked as old as he did! "Harry, we were wondering if you could do anything to make this uniform fit our friend" said Sergeant Brooks, and he handed the bag to Harry who looked at me and then took the uniform out of the bag. After a few seconds, he said "Go upstairs and put it on; leave your clothes up there and let's have a look at you." I was amazed at the amount of old clothes all over the stairs and in the bedroom. If ever he'd had a fire he would never be able to put it out.

When I went down in the uniform, he did not say a word. He just simply took a piece of chalk and marked it all over. "O.K." said Harry, "take it off and put your own clothes back on." When I handed him the uniform, he promptly nicked it all over with a pair of scissors and then started to tear it apart with his bare hands! We thought he was going to ask us to come back next week, but no, he immediately set about it on the old battered sewing machine. After about twenty minutes he placed it back in the bag. "That will be two shillings to you Sergeant" he said. Sergeant Brooks handed him the money and we both thanked him. I could not believe the speed he'd worked to make the uniform fit properly. "I'm going home now," said the Sergeant, "I will see you on Sunday morning with your new uniform on!" I tried it on as soon as I got home. "Blimey" said my mother, "he's made a good job of that – he must be a very good tailor. I'll give it a good pressing before you go on Sunday." On Sunday morning there were lots of comments, mostly in fun, and they all asked if they could take their suits to Harry Cohen!

Over the next three months everything went well in the Home Guard. There was the usual rifle drill and target practice, which I seemed to excel at, and practicing mock invasion tactics, night manoeuvres and parades. Then a bit of a disaster happened which I can now see as very funny, as did many others at the time.

At the top end of Broad Street by Five Ways, there was a café called Kunzles which was a posh place that sold fine coffee and lovely cakes and was well known for its quality. They had a small delivery van with cake racks in the back. They used to loan the van to us when we went on manoeuvres but it was not to be used for troop carrying as it had to be kept clean. We normally used it for carrying weapons and ammunition boxes or for an emergency if anyone was hurt. This particular Sunday morning we marched to the far end of the old Edgbaston Golf Links where there was an old disused building amongst some trees and rough ground, and what at first appeared to be a dried up stream or pond about five feet wide with about two inches of water in it. We had to pretend that the old building was an enemy hide-out and we were to attack it – one section to the left and one section to the right and my section a frontal attack which meant we had to leap over the pond. No problem, we thought, except that my section consisted of quite a few elderly men who were a bit reluctant to jump over this water. We were about thirty yards from the obstacle and we had to run down hill. "Jones" shouted Sergeant-Major Harcourt, "if you can jump over, I'm sure the rest of your section can – care to try it?" "O.K. I'll have a go" I said. I saw no problems especially with only two inches of water, so I took off down the slope with my rifle pointing forward and leapt over alright but then I slipped back down the bank and found myself sinking fast in the middle. Down I went, to my armpits! This was no little stream or pond! The others saw me sinking and pointed a rifle butt at me and said, "Get a hold of this" and two of them managed to drag me out and as I stood on the bank with this dreadful smell drifting about, they all turned away from me holding their noses! This was definitely not a stream or pond – to my horror we discovered that it was an overflow to an old disused CESS PIT!

When it was fully understood by our officer, Lieutenant Wilson, he said, "Get him through the hedge and onto the road. Let's get him home as he cannot march back with us like that." "Driver" he shouted, "get him in the van." The driver of the van shouted back, "I can't have him in here, this is a cake delivery van. I'll get shot if my boss finds out." But he was left with no choice, so he said to me, "Get in the back and don't get near anything – just hang on to those two rails at the top and don't fall over for Christ's sake!" He sat in the driver's seat, very angry, and drove off to my house amidst a lot of cheering and joking. He pulled up outside our front door, opened the back doors of the van and said, "Hurry up; I have to get this cleaned up for Monday." "Stop blooming moaning" I said, "it's me that's in a mess not you" and he drove off very quickly. I walked up the entry hoping no-one would see me and went up to our back door. I tapped on the back window until my mother opened the door and with a gasp said, "What the bloody hell have you done?" She called my Dad, "George come out here, Ron's fallen in the bloody sewer!" My father quite calmly said, "Get in the work shed and strip off." He brought in a large tin bath from the wash house and half filled it with warm water. "Get in there and throw your clothes out" he said. He then hung my uniform on the clothes line and turned the hose on them. After that my mother put them in the wash boiler and scrubbed them clean, then with a further hosing down they came out O.K. After I had cleaned myself up, Dad gave me a bit of a swill down with the hose. No real damage had been done; it had just been a comedy of errors. But we lost the use of the Kunzles cake van. My friends said the customers were complaining about the taste of the cakes!!

The war was still progressing one way and another. Germany had made a big mistake by attacking Russia and was now paying a heavy price at Stalingrad. Men were being slaughtered on both sides but the Russians were getting the advantage. Britain was supplying Russia with armaments in large sea-going convoys and there were times when we too paid a heavy price with the U-boats attacking our ships.

I was just coming up to seventeen years old and one Sunday morning I decided to go to the cinema – after all, apart from watching a funny film, there were the news films which gave us the up-to-date war reports. The cinema was in Bristol Street at the far end, which meant I had to walk about half a mile from my home. As I walked along I saw a young girl in front of me. She was wearing a nice red coat and she looked about my age, my height and quite slim. Most of my friends had girl friends but I was never really drawn towards girls and didn't really have a great deal of confidence to ask girls out. However I plucked up my courage and caught up with this girl and asked her if she was going to the cinema. "Yes" she said, a bit surprised at me asking. "I'm going as well, do you mind if I come with you?" I asked. "No, I don't mind" she replied. To ask a completely strange girl if I could tag along to the cinema was totally out of character for me. We both felt O.K. about it though. After, I walked her home then asked her if I could see her again as I felt quite comfortable about her. She agreed to see me in a couple of weeks time and I was to meet her at the corner of her street. We saw each other on odd occasions but it was nothing serious, just a friendly association. There was never any sexual contact, in fact I had never had any sexual experience with any girl, but that didn't mean I knew nothing about it. In today's modern life it seems to be normal for youngsters to engage in sexual contact at a very early age. I cannot say that I agree with it. In those early days if a young girl was pregnant prior to getting married, most families would hang their heads in shame, but now not so; it seems anything goes.

One week, I met this girl by chance and asked her if we could go to the cinema on Saturday night. "No," she said, "because I have to baby-sit for my little brother as my parents are going out that night." "Oh that's a pity" I said. "But you can come round and sit with us if you like" she replied. Well, I thought, there's nothing else I wanted to do, so I agreed. "Come round at about seven thirty when they go out" she said. Her parents seemed quite friendly. "We will be back at about ten o'clock" they said, and off they went. We sat on the settee, she one end and I on the other with her little brother in the middle. It was difficult to keep him amused for such a long time, but we managed. Eventually he got tired and fell asleep in between us.

The rest of the evening she was showing me photos of her family, which was fine by me. At ten o'clock sharp the door bell rang. "That will be my Mom and Dad, will you let them in Ron?" she asked. As soon as they walked in her mother said, "Everything O.K.?" "Yes, the boy's fast asleep" I said, "but I will have to go now, I think he's made me tired." "Gladys, are you going to make Ron a drink before he goes home?" said her Mom. "O.K." she replied and stood up, but as she did so, to my horror her blasted knickers fell to her feet!! "Oh God!" she said, "that's the second time this week!" I could feel her father's eyes looking at me and I could not get out of the house quickly enough! On the way home I thought, why should I panic, I am perfectly innocent; but it was what her father might be thinking that concerned me. Looking back I can see the funny side of it and put it down to my first sexual experience to see a girl's knickers drop onto her feet! Later on, a few weeks later we both had a good giggle over it.

It was now coming up to late 1942 and I was trying to assess my situation and where I was going. I felt I needed a more interesting job – it seemed as though because of the war, the work was becoming stalemate. It appeared to me that my very practical ability was going unnoticed and the work was becoming too repetitive because of the demand. My education had not been good and I struggled at times with maths and English. I had never been ambitious and I was more content to go along with the stream providing I was happy. The thought of being wealthy never occurred to me but if I think back, none of us had a greedy nature; we were happy to have got through the bad times thanks to our parents.

The war was taking a turn now but terrible news occasionally came over and we were learning of the awful treatment of people by the Germans and the cruelty taking place in concentration camps in and around Germany. However, Germany was now getting a pasting by the R.A.F. and the American Air Force. It was all-out war and no holds barred. The cruelty meted out by one man to another could be described as appalling but this was war, as my father had experienced. At times news would come through that would be uplifting to everyone, giving hope that the war might end more quickly than first thought. Many battles had been fought in North Africa and often it appeared that we were on the losing side over there. The enemy was under the control of Field Marshal Rommel who was respected by General Montgomery who was in charge of the British forces. But now the tide had turned in our favour and eventually the news came that the British had beaten the enemy and run them out of Africa, though of course after the usual loss of lives. Then the call came of a second front which meant that the powerful German military machine had to be beaten on the Continent. I now realized that the war was going on longer than expected and there was a possibility that I might be involved myself, as it would not be long before my eighteenth birthday and that was the call-up age. But whatever happened I intended to enjoy what I could, always remembering my mother's motto, "Laugh at yourself if there's nothing else to laugh at." Strange things always seemed to happen in my life no matter how serious the situation; something stupid would happen which in later life gave rise to laughter. Perhaps this is what my mother meant.

I thought more and more of the probability of my being called up as it didn't look at all likely that the war would end before my eighteenth birthday. I preferred the R.A.F. as I had always had a very strong interest in aircraft from a very young age. I made several models of war planes; a Spitfire, a Hawker Hurricane and others. I had an understanding of the theory of flight after reading books on how something so heavy could fly. My biggest disappointment was that I knew I would never become part of the air crew owing to my poor education – partly my own fault as lots of things at school didn't interest me.

CHAPTER FIVE

In everybody's life there are changes and, like going round a bend in a river, things become so different. I realize now that I was a bit naïve and took things for granted. I came home from work one day in January 1943, feeling tired as usual. "There's a brown envelope from the War Ministry arrived this morning for you – I think it's your call-up papers" my mother said quietly. I had a quick glance at it before I cleaned myself up then sat down to read it as I drank a cup of tea. "Oh, I've got to go the Army Recruiting Office for a medical, it says – but I want to go into the R.A.F." I said, sounding a bit disappointed. "You may not have any choice" Mom replied. When Dad walked in from work I asked him, "Can I choose which part of the services I want to go in?" "I don't think so during war time; they put you in whatever they think you are suitable for after checking on you." He picked up the letter and looked at it. "Yes it looks as if you are for the Army anyway, according to this."

That evening I went out to see one of my pals to tell him. Dougie was an old school friend of mine who only lived a couple of hundred yards down the street. He was a jolly kid and easily pleased. "I've had my call-up papers and have to go for an examination for the Army" I told him, "but I'm a bit disappointed as I wanted to go in the R.A.F." "That's funny, I had mine a few days ago for the Navy, but that's O.K. by me as I always wanted the Navy!" he said. "You jammy bugger!" I exclaimed. "We will have to write to each other when we go away" I suggested. "That's a good idea, let's go and have a drink on that" was his reply. So off we went and ended up in our local pub and had a long friendly chat and hoped all went well for us both. We then said goodnight and shook hands. It was another nine months before I saw him again, and that was by sheer chance.

A few days later I had half a day off from work and walked to the Army Recruiting Office. A sergeant at the door directed me where to go and wait with the others. There were about twenty five young chaps waiting, and as our names were called out in turn, we had to go into a smaller room. I don't think I was there for more than a couple of minutes. "Ron Jones next" called the man in the other room. "Take off your jacket and shirt" he said. This man was to medically examine me – he wasn't in uniform or in a white coat as most doctors are. He gave me an eye test first then looked at my teeth. Next he put a stethoscope on my chest then went down below and asked me to cough. "Do you have any trouble with your feet?" he asked, "like corns or blisters or athletes foot?" "No, never" I said. "Right, put your clothes back on. You will be getting instructions where to go, and a railway warrant for travel. You are A.1. fit for the Army." "Could you say which branch of the Army I will be in?" I asked him. "That's up to the Army to decide when they get my report" he replied. So out I walked. That was really a whirlwind examination, probably less than twenty minutes from the time of my arrival. So that's what the Army is going to be like, I thought to myself, and feeling a bit confused I walked home.

The following day I reported to my boss, Mr. Roberts. "I've had my call-up papers from the Army" I told him. "But I can defer you" he replied. "What, altogether?" I asked. "No, I can defer you for six months as you are on war work, and then another six months after that" he said. "No, thanks – I will go when I'm called which will only be at the most in two weeks time. I'm a bit disappointed that I can't go into the R.A.F. but there's nothing I can do about it" I said.

However, as many times in the past, fate alters the course of things in a peculiar way. A few days later, I had a bit of an accident with my right arm. It didn't seem much as it only broke the skin, so I didn't bother to get it treated, but after a few days it began to turn bad ways and my arm started to swell up and go stiff. At the end of the week my arm had really swollen up badly and a lump had appeared under my arm. The following Saturday afternoon my father looked at it and said, "I'm afraid it's the hospital for you! I'll take you up when I have changed into clean clothes." This meant the local Accident Hospital which I knew well as I had been in it a few times as a kid. "Right, off we go" said my Dad. We had to walk as there was no such thing as hopping into the car then, as no-one had cars!

There was a brief examination by the doctor who said, "I'm afraid we shall have to operate on that arm tonight as it's full of poison. Leave

30

him with us and send someone to collect him tomorrow night." He took me upstairs where I waited for about half an hour in a corridor. Then another doctor appeared and said, "Come with me, lad." He took me into a room where I had been before. There was a small operating table in the middle of the room. "Take off your jacket, shirt and boots" he said, "and lie on the table. I'm going to put a needle into your wrist and I want you to count from one to twenty." "Yes, I know" I said. "So you have been here before, then?" he asked. "Yes doctor" I replied. "O.K. then, just lie still." I think I only got to about twelve, then I was gone.

I don't know how long I had been asleep when I suddenly sat bolt upright with a terrible burning sensation in my arm. Immediately I felt a swab stinking of ether pushed into my face and I was off again. I came round at about midnight and was lying on a bed with my socks and trousers still on, and my arm was heavily bandaged. "Would you like a cup of tea?" someone said. I just answered "Yes" to whoever it was but I must have gone straight off again as it was still there at eight o'clock the next morning. I was offered food, but refused as I felt so sick. I think I must have been asleep for the rest of the day.

"Your sister has come to collect you" said the nurse, "so you can get up now." My sister helped me with my jacket and boots. "You will have to bring him back on Tuesday afternoon about two o'clock" the nurse told my sister, and off we went home.

"How's your arm?" Mother asked. "It's O.K. very sore but O.K. I have to go back on Tuesday for some more treatment" I told her. I did nothing much until Tuesday, wondering what on earth they'd done to me. Returning to the hospital, the nurse cut the bandage off and I was able to see that they had cut a large slit in my arm and packed it with some sort of lint and a small rubber tube to drain the fluid. After my arm had been cleaned out it was re-packed and re-bandaged and another doctor came and promptly started to cover my whole arm with plaster whilst it was in the bent position. When it was set solid, he said, "Come back in two weeks time and we will take the plaster off. You can go now."

"What the bloody hell have they put that plaster on for!" exclaimed my mother when I walked back into the house. "I've got to keep it in this position so that the cut will not keep moving as it has to drain" I said. "Well you can't go in the Army like that" she said – something I hadn't thought about. Typical of my mother, she wrote a letter to whoever was in charge at the recruiting office, explaining that her son could not be called up yet as his arm was in plaster and he wouldn't be able to fire a rifle! I was amazed that she had put that in the letter! A few days later another brown envelope arrived explaining that any problem I had would be treated by Army Medical personnel and enclosed were full instructions to report to Copthorne Barracks in Shrewsbury on the following Monday at one o'clock. Also enclosed was the railway warrant to go from New Street station to Shrewsbury station. "That Copthorne Barracks is an Infantry training place" said my father. "Just my bloody luck," I said to him, "and I'm beginning with my arm in plaster – that's a bad omen for a start!" I was well aware that in the First World War it was the Infantry which lost the most men, but it was no good thinking about that now. My brother piped up by saying, "You're going to look a right one when you walk into the barracks with your little brown suitcase and your arm in plaster!" (My brother had been deferred for twelve months but had since been called up and was in the Royal Army Service Corps and was on leave).

On the Saturday my mother sorted out a small brown leather suitcase for me complete with odds and ends like a toothbrush, a bit of soap and a towel and there was space for a cheese sandwich. My parents came with me to see me off and to my surprise there were about half a dozen other young lads standing on the platform, they obviously had been called up as well. I walked up to one chap who was standing on his own and asked, "Where are you off too then?" "The same as those others over there, Copthorne Barracks, Shrewsbury. What's the matter with your arm?" he asked. "Oh I've had an operation on it" I said. "You're lucky then; if it had been left to the Army, they would have chopped the bloody thing off – they don't mess about, my older brother reckons!" he replied. "You'll do well in the Army, cheering us all up!" I said, but it was just a joking remark. Then the train pulled in and all seven of us piled into the same coach. I think it cheered us up to be together. Our parents all wished us well as the train moved forward with a clanging sound, and with waving arms through the window, the train slipped away.

CHAPTER SIX

The train picked up speed and we were on our way. "Goodbye New Street station" I said, "I spent a lot of time at that station as a small boy, watching the huge steam engines!" At that, we all got chatting, and hoped that we'd stay together in the Army as we were all Brummies. After a while one lad said, "Just look at that beautiful countryside." We gazed out of the window and yes, it was – the Shropshire countryside was wonderful with rolling hills all nice and green. "You wouldn't think there was a war on would you?" said another, "I suppose this is what they mean when they say we are to fight for King and Country – and they are worth fighting for." One tall lad leaned out of the window and said, "I can see a town in the distance; I wonder if anyone will be on the station to meet us?" "I would think so," I replied, "but we can always ask where the Barracks are.

The train started to slow down but it still took a good fifteen minutes to get into the station, and with a squeal of the brakes it came to a standstill. "Shrewsbury station" a porter shouted. We stumbled out of the carriage feeling a bit apprehensive. "I can't see anyone that looks military, but I can see the way out over there," said one of the lads, so we walked through the gate and found ourselves on what appeared to be the main street. "Go up the hill, over the river bridge then turn left" said a complete stranger who had obviously seen little groups like ours before. "O.K. thank you" we said. This little uphill street was quite pretty and as we went along we looked all about us. "What a nice place," one commented. About two hundred yards up the hill I spotted a little pub on the left. "Hey wait lads, we've plenty of time – how about us having a drink together in that pub?" I suggested. One or two of them were a bit reluctant but after a bit of encouragement they all agreed. We went into a very small bar and all had half a pint each. "This is the life," someone said, and we all agreed that we were going to get some fun out of being here together for a while. After about ten minutes, the door clicked open and in walked an Army Sergeant. "Right you lot, there's a truck outside, so finish your drinks and get into the truck as soon as possible – you're ten minutes late already" he said. Some of us pretended to look at our wrist-watches which we hadn't got. Then we all scrambled into the back of the lorry and I struggled because of my arm being set at right-angles, but the Sergeant didn't say anything as I don't think he even noticed my problem. Perhaps that's what Army life is going to be like, I thought. The Sergeant got in the front with the driver and off we went. It wasn't long before we crossed the river bridge and everything looked so nice. We carried on for another five minutes then we suddenly turned sharp right into the Barracks, where there was a smart soldier on guard at the gate. "Look at this lot" said one of the chaps, "all the bloody stones are painted white!" Then I remembered someone saying to me, "When you're in the Army, if it moves salute it, if it doesn't, then white-wash it!" Looks like that here, I thought.

The truck stopped and we were told to get out and stand in a line by a hut which I noticed was the Quartermaster's Stores. I also noticed another group of recruits which had arrived from a different part of the country. A young Officer came up to talk to us. "You will now be issued with a full set of Army clothing which you will take with you to Hut No.3 (which he pointed to), choose your own bunk bed of which there are twenty four, then put on your Army clothes and put your civilian clothes into the bags provided. Right men, let's get started." In single file we walked into the Stores where there was a long table and three N.C.O.'s handing out the uniforms etc. They just checked our height and asked us our shoe size and that was all. In turn they issued us with everything; tunic, trousers, boots, socks, shirts etc., and finally piled a tin hat on top of the bundle. We then walked over to Hut 3 where Army life was to start. But something was bothering me – I had seen an Officer, two Sergeants, three N.C.O.'s and not one of them questioned me about the bloody great chunk of plaster holding my arm at right-angles! However, now I had the real opportunity for someone to take note. "Sergeant" I said, "I can't put the tunic on because of my plastered arm – I would have to cut the sleeve off." He gave a quick look at my arm and said, "Oh yes, of course, right come with me." He walked me over the parade ground to a small building showing a red cross. A young Medical Officer sat at a desk inside. "Could you have a look at this man Sir?" he asked. "Right, and what has been the trouble with your arm, lad?" I gave a brief description and he said, "Alright Sergeant, I will send him over when I've looked at his arm." He sat me down and took a large pair of scissors and started to hack away at the plaster, eventually removed it all and carefully took off the bandage and the packing in the wound. "Come over here" he called to his two colleagues, "come and look at what a lovely job they have done on his arm." He took out the tubing and cleaned up my arm and bandaged it up again. "O.K. lad, it will be alright now, just give it a few days to heal completely. You can go back to your pals now." I walked back to the Hut thinking what he had said about it being a good job and wondering what the Army would have done.

When we were all dressed in our uniforms, I realised that I would still have trouble with my arm as it was still very stiff. The Sergeant in charge called us outside as the Officer was to give us a short talk. He looked left and right at us and said, "Right men, I welcome you all to Copthorne Barracks. You will be here for approximately four months and you will be trained in self-discipline, comradeship and weaponry. Without discipline an army fails, but it's not going to happen here. I'm sure you'll all enjoy your training and on completion of that you will be posted to your Regiments. Now you can dismiss and be taken to the mess for some dinner. Thank you." A bit of a cheer went up at that. After our food we went back to Hut 3 where the Sergeant in charge came in and gave us a brief run-down of the rules, times of reveille, meals and parades etc. He then left us to ourselves to relax for a while after this very important day in all of our lives.

We sorted out our kit and made our beds, then we gathered at one end of the room sitting on anybody's bed and chatted, getting to know each other as after all we now had to learn to live with one another and get used to the others habits and characters. Eventually "lights out" was sounded and we slipped between our blankets with our own thoughts and worries. I knew I could cope with the hardships but we all knew there was a lot to do to turn us into real soldiers.

The following morning the Sergeant came and pushed the door open with a "Wakey-wakey" call and left the door wide open letting in the cold air. We had a quick clean up with cold water, dressed and went off to the mess for a breakfast of toast and fish cakes and a mug of tea. This was obviously going to be the routine for the next twelve weeks. At breakfast the Sergeant announced we were to be on parade outside the hut at nine o'clock where we would be inspected and asked questions. We went back to our quarters as quickly as possible, folded our blankets, tidied up and polished our boots. On parade another Sergeant stood in front and ordered us to stand to attention, then proceeded to ask questions in turn, e.g. what was our religion, who were our next of kin and the type of work we did in civilian life. All this was written down for future records. Then he read out our individual Army number, emphasising that we must learn and remember it as we may be asked this at any time. We were then told to be back on parade in half an hour, stripped to the waist to start our exercise lessons to get us fit. When he returned we were already jumping up and down as it was so cold. We were ordered to get into single file and to run round the parade ground twenty times at a steady pace. Fitness, he told us, is essential to an Infantry soldier. A lot of the boys didn't make it, but this was what it was all about now, seeing who could do what. After the run, we had a shower before having our lunch. Everything was constantly impressed upon us like fitness, smartness and cleanliness. After lunch at two thirty, we had to parade again this time fully dressed and smart as we were to have two hours of constant drill to "knock us into shape" as he put it. Occasionally someone would turn right instead of left which caused a bit of laughter. We would immediately get a rollicking from the Sergeant but after a while we seemed to get the hang of it. "That was quite good," said the Sergeant "but you will be much better before you leave here." We were then allowed to go back to our Hut to rest a little before a late tea. After that we were left to ourselves and we talked about the day and ended up telling each other jokes.

Next day, a Wednesday, things seemed to be better and getting more interesting although at this stage we were not yet allowed to handle weapons for safety reasons. We were shown them and had them demonstrated – rifles, mortars, machine guns, hand-grenades etc. It kept us occupied as we knew soon we would have to practice with them for real. However, amongst all these serious things there always seemed to be something that can be remembered as funny.

On the Friday of the second week, we were ordered to be on parade outside the Medical Office for our inoculations. We were to be stripped to the waist with our hands on our hips and had to walk in single file through the door of the building where upon two young medics stuck needles into our arms on each side, each of us getting three injections for various diseases. We were then told to walk straight through and go back to our Hut where we could have the rest of the day off duty. As we all lay on our bunks, slowly most of the chaps' arms started to swell up and give them discomfort. All you could hear was, "Look at my bloody arm how swollen it is!" "It's not as bad as mine" another would say. The funny thing was that I had no discomfort at all with mine and later, as the others were groaning and complaining, I went outside to the toilets. On the way back I thought I would play a joke on them.

I opened the door a small way and shouted as a sergeant would, "Right you lot, get your kit on and go outside on parade!" To my surprise not a sound came out of the hut. Then the door slowly opened wide and to my horror the Sergeant was standing in the doorway. "So, you're feeling rather frisky are you Jones?" "No Sergeant" I replied. "Well lad, get your kit on straight away" he ordered. I had obviously put my foot in it! With all my kit on and carrying a pile of tin hats, he made me run round the Parade Ground six times. I learned a good lesson – keep my bloody mouth shut!

I have always accepted the fact that I was a little on the clumsy side, and again on the following Friday I was in a bit of bother. Since we had been on the camp none of us had been allowed out to walk around Shrewsbury, but after another week of discipline and training it was announced that we were to have our first pay parade and time off, and although my arm was healing now, it was still quite stiff and I found it quite awkward to salute properly for which I was always being told off. The procedure for getting paid was for the Sergeant in charge to call your name and number from his list, and you would then step forward, salute the Officer and put out your left hand to receive the cash, turn to the left and walk away. Well, I thought, I must get my salute right this time at least as my arm was much easier. The Sergeant called out a few names and then it was my turn. "Next," he called, "Jones 630" (he just used the last three numbers). I stepped forward smartly and shot my right arm out as far as it would go to salute. Disaster! My hand knocked the clip-board straight out of his hand – his list of names went under the table, so I bent down to pick it up. "STAND STILL!" he bawled out. "Sorry Sergeant, but you were standing too close to me." I said. "QUIET MAN!" he shouted out again in a rage. I could hear muffled laughter at the back of me and the Officer put his head in his hands whilst the Sergeant rattled off his orders to the lads to be quiet. When the pay parade was over, he kept us standing then proceeded to walk along the line looking at each man in the eye and when he got to me he stared at me for what seemed five minutes then said, "Jones, I will have to keep my eye on you." He then dismissed us.

The incident was soon forgotten as more interesting news was coming for us. However, before that, a little bit of sad news came the following week when two of the twenty four lads had to leave us, John and Ben. John unfortunately was a hairless man, he had no hair on his body, head, eyebrows or anywhere. He thought that he would eventually be a subject of ridicule and requested that he was posted to a branch of the Military Police, which was granted. Ben was a tall thin Black Country boy and was constantly home-sick and couldn't cope, so he was transferred to a Military Despatch department, like a large stores, which meant that he would never go abroad. We wished them both good luck.

A few days later we were driven through a small pretty village called Church Stretton. We ended up at the foot of a range of hills called the Long Mynd where there was a shooting range. We spent most of the day there and it was very enjoyable as I could shoot quite accurately as I had done in the Home Guard, so I was quite pleased. Afterwards we were driven back to our barracks, given a good supper and we spent the rest of the evening in our Hut enjoying ourselves having a good laugh and joke.

Some of them talked about their ambitions in the Army but I didn't really have any ambitions at all. I suppose I was a bit of a lazy person and I never did change. I have always believed in the saying that a leopard never changes his spots – we might modify our lives but deep down we remain the same.

Later that week we all had to go into a very large building where we were to be shown the workings of Army trucks and tracked vehicles. This I revelled in as I had read about vehicle engineering in my earlier days and found it fascinating. Lots of components from engines and transmissions lay on benches, and these parts were shown and described to us, then we were asked questions about them. I think I answered 90% of my questions correctly. "Did you work in a garage?" asked the instructor. "No, I was a toolmaker" I replied. The next morning there were six names on the notice board for taking a drivers' course and my name was on it so I was again very pleased. There was also notification that we were to be allowed out at the weekends providing we were on our best behaviour and we were to be inspected for smartness before we could leave the camp. The first time out was on the next Sunday after lunch. As we walked out the Sergeant was by the gate checking our uniform and he said, "Back at nine o'clock you lot." It was a really nice sunny afternoon and we walked to the river bridge where there was a path and benches along side, so we all sat there for a while appreciating the freedom and the scenery and some of us talked about fishing the river.

The next Wednesday morning the six of us who were to have driving lessons had to be on parade on the square at 9.30 whereupon a truck driven by the instructor showed up. "Now" he said, "I want five of you in the back and one in the front with me. You, Jones, in first." He talked me through the procedures of the controls then drove the truck round the square telling me everything he was doing. Coming to a halt he said, "Right, now let's see what you can do – but not too fast!" I drove around for about ten minutes then the other chaps had their turns. "Now let's start again but this time out on the road" said the instructor. I climbed into the driver's seat again and he told me to go slowly through the gate and turn left into the town. We went over the river bridge, turned left again and down the High Street, the instructor telling me which road to take until we ended up outside the Barracks again. He never made a comment only for me to get out and send the next chap in. When all six of us had repeated this exercise the only words he spoke were, "Right, dismiss – same time tomorrow." Back at the Hut, the others had been square-bashing (marching drill) so there were a few fruity comments like "you lucky bastards!" but we all got on

O.K. whatever jobs we did. The following morning as arranged we six gathered on the square. The instructor walked over – but where was the truck? "Follow me" he said and he led us past a building and out through a gate, and there was a shiny new Bren gun carrier. We just stood open mouthed! "This is a bit different to steer" he said, then explained why and what we had to do. This was all about the use of the brakes and the differential drive shaft. We were to go through the same procedure as with the truck but not out onto the street. The six of us spent all day getting the hang of it but we seemed to do O.K. We were late back for our tea but we didn't mind.

The next day we all had to do a long route march and we were shattered when we got back but luckily the Mess had saved us a late dinner and then we had the rest of the evening to ourselves. The following day we had to hand in our pay books and a bit more good news came when we were given back our pay books as they had now been marked with various things for different men. The six of us who had been driving had ours stamped with our qualification as drivers for trucks and track laying vehicles. That weekend we were allowed out on Saturday and Sunday.

Later the next week we were told we could all have a pass and railway warrant to go home for the weekend. The Army was now looking good for us and we could hardly wait for the Friday to come. However, they did put us through it for the rest of the week – rifle drill, physical training, running whilst carrying our rifles over our heads etc. At last Friday came and our passes were handed to us at mid-afternoon although we couldn't leave for home before four thirty. We were all jumping about like kids needing the toilet and when the Sergeant spotted us at about four fifteen he said, "Oh go on then, but don't forget to come back!" We were off like a shot to see who could be first to the station. I wanted to go to New Street station for Birmingham and others were going to Coventry, Wolverhampton, and a couple of Welsh boys were going to Cardiff.

I arrived home at about eight thirty and walked into the house shouting "Hello Mom!" "What are you doing home?" she asked with a puzzled look on her face. I'm sure she thought I had absconded. "I've got a weekend pass" I said, "and I'm going to get one more often now. Where's Dad and my brother?" "Your brother is in Italy now and your

Dad's gone for a drink down the road." I dashed out again straight to Dad's regular Pub. "Hello Dad" I said. He looked at me, very surprised. "How are you son, I was wondering when they would give you a leave." "I've just seen Mom and I think she thought I had absconded" I told him. "Well she has been worried about you all the time" he said.

How great it was to get into my old bed with sheets! I went to bed at ten thirty and didn't wake up until eleven thirty on the Saturday morning. When I got up Mom said, "I've never known you get up that late on a Saturday – what the devil have they been doing to you?" "It's O.K. Mom, everything's fine, and I've got my driving licence now. It's tough but enjoyable." "Good" she said. "I spoke to your Dad last night and we are going to have a little party for you, so get your friends to come round if you want. Dorothy (she's my eldest sister) is married now so she is coming but her husband can't because he's on duty." So I went out to round up my friends including a couple of girls who worked with my younger sister. My Dad fetched a few bottles of beer and some lemonade and Mom fixed up some food and that was it – all set! As expected a good time was had by all and my father sang some of his comical army songs. I'd had a lovely weekend with my family and friends. That was going to be the pattern now for the next six weeks.

CHAPTER SEVEN

Back at the Barracks things seemed to be winding down a bit. There was a mood in the air that they were getting us ready for posting to the various regiments. One morning we were on parade and we were told which branch of the Infantry we were being sent to. I, with about fifteen others, was going north to join the King's Shropshire Light Infantry and we were to leave on the following Tuesday from Shrewsbury station. A young Officer was to escort us but we were never told exactly where we were going – it was all kept secret. On Monday evening we were all ready and a large box of rations was prepared so we reckoned we would be on the train for some time. After breakfast on that Tuesday, we were loaded into a large truck with all our gear. There was a great deal of speculation as to where we would end up. I reckoned we were all going to miss Copthorne. When we arrived at the station the Officer told us to form into three groups and stand well back as the train was coming in. The compartments held eight people but as we had all our gear with us the Officer put five in each. The whistle blew and off we went. I think we were all a bit apprehensive and kept constantly talking, but the Officer didn't disclose anything. The train itself never seemed to get up to full speed and stopped at every station; first Whitchurch then Crewe where we changed trains but were there for an hour. Next came Wigan and Preston. There were lots of military personnel coming and going and each station had a couple of N.A.A.F.I. girls dishing out free tea to them. At Penrith we got off the train as it had to stop again for half an hour, so we had our sandwiches and a mug of tea. We then hopped back onto the train wondering where on earth we were going. We passed through Carlisle which told us we were nearly in Scotland and we had been travelling for about seven hours including all the stops.

The Officer came through to each compartment to tell us that we would be disembarking at the next station which was Lockerbie. "Make sure you do not leave anything behind before you get out" he said. "Lockerbie, that's out in the bloody wild!" someone commented. It was a very tiny station, but for all that a couple of N.A.A.F.I. girls were there to offer us a drink. But there was no time to spare as we were running very late. An Army lorry was parked on the road. "Where the bloody hell have you lot been?" shouted the driver. We were herded into the back, the Officer in the front, and we were off.

It was getting dark quite quickly and it was very overcast. It was about four miles to the camp. We slowed down, turned right over the River Annan (the river actually ran through the camp), and we pulled up outside a large wooden building. "Everyone dismount and form a line in front of the Dining Hall" an Officer ordered. This we did whilst looking around at this so different place. We then went inside the Dining Hall where the Battalion Commander briskly walked in and stood on a stool to say a few words to us. "Gentlemen" he started, (a whisper from one of the men, "Blimey that's a bit different from hey you lot!") "I wish to welcome you all to the Second Battalion of the King's Shropshire Light Infantry Regiment, a Regiment which used to be called the 85th Foot Regiment, and it has a fine history of war records. It is probably one of the finest known Infantry Regiments I am proud to say. We wish you to keep up that fine record. Thank you Gentlemen" he finished.

We were then quickly marched to the row of men's quarters. The Sergeant had a list of names and called mine out first. "Jones you are allotted to No.1 Hut." He continued calling out names and it appeared that I would be in a different hut to all the others. This was very disappointing to me as I would not be with anyone I knew. An N.C.O. came over to me and said, "Come with me mate" and took me to the Stores. It was already dark now. "There's a folding bed there – grab hold of it and three blankets and I'll take you to Hut 1." he said. I was beginning to feel a bit low by this time, and was told to sort myself a bed space and to fetch my equipment. Inside the Hut were two rows of bunks where some of the men were reading or writing and others just sitting chatting and smoking. But where was this bed space? There wasn't one! Then I caught the eye of a chap lying on his bunk and he looked sympathetically at me. "Are you O.K. mate?" he asked. "No, I'm looking for this bloomin' bed space that's supposed to be here." I replied. "We're not very organized yet" he remarked, but he promptly got up and moved his bed over and the chap's next to him which gave me a space. I placed my bed down with the blankets and went to fetch my gear. Outside it was very quiet as everyone had gone. When I went back inside, the friendly chap told me his name was Harry and he came from Bideford in Devon. "My name is Ron and I'm from Birmingham" I said. "Yes, I thought you were," he replied. Then he told me about the selection of men in the Hut – a few Welsh guys, some from the Midlands, some from Yorkshire, in fact all over the country. "Some are regular soldiers and some are ex-Dunkirk chaps in fact a lot of them have long service," he said. Somehow I was beginning to feel out of place here and I was wishing I was back at Copthorne. I think he had noticed I wasn't happy. "Don't worry Ron, we were all in the same situation to start with. I should make your bed up if I were you, it will be lights out soon. I'll wake you up in the morning and show you where to go for washing etc, and take you to the Mess for our breakfast." After lying awake for a while feeling very apprehensive and uncertain I eventually dropped off. It had come to me on our long journey that this was not going to be like Copthorne. This was going to be a long slow bend in that river of life which would give me a great deal of experience.

It did not seem very long before Harry was tugging at me. "Come on kid, the bugle's gone" he said quietly. Stripped to the waist we both followed the others to the ablutions. "How on earth do you do this every morning? It's bloody freezing out here!" I said. The ablutions block was for washing and was just a row of sinks with a tin roof on top and there was no hot water. I always believed I could cope with harsh conditions after my hard up-bringing but I knew, like the other lads, that there was nothing we could do but our best. After dressing, we had a brisk walk over to the Mess – everyone in a queue holding out their mess tins into which was dropped a fried fish cake, a boiled egg, a sausage and a crust of bread. "Harry, this looks pretty good" I said as I was handed a mug of tea as well. "Don't be too optimistic, it will probably be salty porridge for the next two weeks!" he replied.

In the Hut was now a complete Platoon. In a Battalion there are four Rifle Companies totalling six hundred and twenty men, also a support Company with Mortar guns and anti-tank weapons, and an H.Q. Company. Each Rifle Company is divided into Platoons and each Platoon divided into three sections. Now with our arrival the Battalion was up to full strength and would now start the real training as we had been told we would be taking an important part in the awaited call for the Second Front, but what and where they could not disclose.

That morning the Platoon was called on parade at nine o'clock with our rifles. We stood in three ranks to be inspected – most of us being criticised for something! We had drill for one and a half hours then were dismissed to clean our rifles, then back on parade for rifle inspection. After lunch, back on parade at two o'clock – another quick inspection then we had to march out of the camp for about a mile up the road. I found the marching speed was exceptionally fast, in fact I learned later that the K.S.L.I. marched faster than most of the other Infantry Regiments. We turned left up a well-worn lane towards a rather large steep hill covered in bracken. When we started up the hill we broke ranks and in single file had to go to the top and down the other side. This was a bit of an endurance test, the problem being the wet bracken and all sorts of wild shrubs; consequently our trousers were soon soaking wet. At the bottom of the hill we came onto another track and turned right. "Halt" called the Sergeant, "Form into two columns then quick march back to the Camp," which was now about five miles away. On arrival we were dismissed and told to go back to our quarters. "Thank God that's over" I said to Harry. "I'm afraid there's a lot worse to come than that!" he replied. We dried out the best we could around the coke fire in the middle of the Hut. After our tea we had the rest of the evening to ourselves. I was feeling a bit better now as I was chatting to some of the lads and getting to know their names. One chap was Jewish named Josh Abrahams; he was always trying to get extras in the Mess.

While we were lying on our bunks relaxing, a young Officer came in and started asking one of the lads some questions. The lad seemed to be getting a bit up tight and the Officer lost his temper. "What's all that about?" I asked Harry. "I'll give you a tip," he said, "steer clear of him – he's a Bastard." I was surprised at what he said. "Just wait and see – you'll find out." He obviously knew something I didn't know.

The River Annan ran through the Camp. It was a trout river that was not very deep but when we had some rain it ran very fast. At the far end there were two ropes right across the river and secured to strong posts either side. One morning all the Companies had to strip to the waist and with only our trousers and boots on we all walked in single file to the ropes, then by holding onto one of the ropes we had to wade across the river making sure we did not loose the rope as we could be swept away. The second rope was a few yards down stream for us to grab hold in case we loosed the first rope. The water was like ice. The Platoon Sergeant went over first and we followed, all making it over to the other side. We then ran along the bank to go over the foot-bridge and back to the Huts where we were allowed to stay and get dry. We were not asked to do anything else that day. Later I noticed that same Officer coming into the Hut and asking more questions. I looked at Harry and he just winked at me. "You'll see" he said. I was still puzzled.

The training seemed to be stepping up and getting tougher and not only that, the demand for doing everything faster. There seemed to be an unease about the Company and I couldn't put my finger on it, but at Copthorne I had learned to keep my mouth shut. The following evening while we were relaxing, a Corporal who I recognised from the other Platoon, came in with a list of names on a large sheet of paper. In turn he went to every chap in the Hut who signed it, but when he passed me he just looked and remarked, "Not you mate," it was obviously because I was new to it all. I just cast an eye at Harry and he put his finger to his lips – in other words say nought.

The next evening it all came out that the Corporal with the list of all the men in our Company had gone to see the Battalion Commander and calmly said to him, "All the men on this list, Sir, have refused to follow Officer……. into action." When I found out, I realised that this was mutiny at the highest level. If the Corporal had done this in the First World War he would certainly have been shot – but every man in the Company was with him and recognised him as being a very brave man and they wouldn't let him down. It took a lot for it to sink in that it was happening in the British Army. The Officer concerned disappeared the next day; he must have been transferred somewhere but we never got to know – it was obviously all hushed up and no more was said.

The following day we did some mountain climbing. On part of the track was a crevice about six feet deep with a small stream at the bottom. We were walking along the edge of this and I was just admiring the view and not paying attention when I tripped and slipped down the crevice. After a slight telling off, the chaps gave me a pull out but I had hurt my ankle. When we got back at about four o'clock I sat on my bunk and asked one of the lads what the procedure was for seeing the Medical Officer. "That's easy", he said, "but make sure you have a genuine case to see him as he hates scroungers." "I think I really damaged my ankle when I fell" I replied. "Well, that's up to you" he said. So I decided it would be O.K. by morning and I would say nothing. But the following morning my ankle had swollen up. However I still said nothing as there wasn't anything on that was important that day. Then about ten o'clock a Sergeant came in and detailed twelve of us to march to a farm about three miles away. The farmer supplied us with spuds and about half a ton had to be loaded onto his tractor trailer. Obviously we were to march rather than casually walk and we had only gone about a quarter of a mile but I couldn't keep up because of my ankle. "Halt" shouted the Sergeant. "What's up with your foot, Jones?" "I hurt it yesterday while we up the mountain" I told him. "Why the hell didn't you report to the Medic!" he bellowed, and immediately sent me back to have it looked at. That's another clanger I've dropped, I thought. I went straight to the Medical Office and was examined by the M.O. who gave me seven days excused duty! I had damaged my ankle much worse than I thought. So I had nothing to do for a week and no-one could give me orders as I had a ticket which, I was told by my fellow Platoon chaps, was difficult to get. "Scrounging bastard!" one said jokingly. I just laughed at him and lay back on my bunk!

One of the things we regularly had to do was to look at the notice board to see if our names were listed for any special duties. On one evening my name was there. Evidently I had been chosen with ten others to be tested for a radio course. This was a big disappointment to me as I had no interest in radio at all. "How can I get off this?" I asked the lads. "You can't" said one of the older ones, "just go and have the test and make a muck-up of the writing and spelling. They won't have you if your English if bad." Good idea, I thought. The test wasn't for another couple of weeks.

We had heard that a new replacement Officer was arriving – Lieutenant Gwilliam. There was a noticeable difference now in the morale of the Company, and the lads were much happier. When Lieutenant Gwilliam arrived, he came and introduced himself to us; he seemed a real gentleman and arranged to take us on a local march through the quiet countryside to see how we were getting on and to get to know us.

So the next day we assembled on the edge of the Parade ground and stood to attention. "Right gentlemen, it's a nice day so we will go on a brisk march and I'm sure you'll enjoy the route I have picked for you." We started off through the gate and over the river bridge. Instead of turning left towards Lockerbie we turned right through the village of Eclesfechan, then turned left into very nice quiet countryside. We were going at a brisk pace for a while, but Lt. Gwilliam who was at the front started to slow down then walked at the side of the column. "Don't you ever sing when you're out like this?" he asked the Corporal. "Very rarely" was the reply. "Right, then let's start – let's have 'It's a Long Way to Tipperary'" he said. Within the next hundred yards every man was singing in time to the marching, and continued on through all the old First World War songs. This was really something that boosted our optimism and morale. After about five miles we stopped by a wood where a lot of tree felling had taken place. "We will have a break now and those who wish to smoke may do so" said Lt. Gwilliam. We all sat on the old tree trunks and talked whilst the Lt. asked some of us our names. After about half an hour, we were on the way back and in time for lunch. Yes, it was a good few hours out, we all agreed. We were not required to do any more for the rest of the day. There now seemed to be a complete change of atmosphere, and we also agreed that this new man was no fool and would not let the discipline deteriorate.

Periodically when I was in the Mess, especially at tea time, I would come into contact with few of the lads I joined up with. There was Bob Williams, Taffy Hughes, and the Jewish lad Josh Abrahams. Two of them were in the same Company but in different Platoons. One tea time they asked me if I fancied going into Lockerbie at six thirty. "Is that alright?" I asked. "Yes it's O.K. providing we have no further duties in the evening and make sure that we book out at the gate, but we must be back by eleven o'clock." "Right then I'll come with you" I said. We met up as arranged at the gate, booked out then set off. "It's about five and a half miles" remarked Taffy so we started to stride it out. We'd gone about half a mile when an H.Q. lorry pulled up. "Where are you off to" called the driver. "Lockerbie" we all shouted. "Hop in, I'm going to the station to pick up some gear" he said. What a relief from walking, I thought. "I've never walked around Lockerbie only passed through it" I said. "Oh it's alright, at least there's a Pub, a Fish shop and a very small cinema" Bob said.

The driver dropped us off near the railway station and we thanked him. "Best of luck lads" he called. "Let's have a look at the cinema first" I said, so we headed straight there. The thought of going to the Pub and then having to walk all the way back was a bad idea we agreed. The film for that night was Emlyn Williams in "Hatters Castle" – I've never had difficulty in remembering that! We thought a good relaxing sit down watching the film was ideal. Afterwards we headed for the Fish Shop, but the owner was just about to close when we walked in. "What did you want, lads?" he asked. "Oh, just some chips and a pickled egg each" we said. "Can you wait fifteen minutes?" "Yes, fine" we replied. We were very pleased and thanked the man, who gave us a couple of pickled onions as well. We all thought it was great and set off eating our chips. It was a long walk back but we had plenty to talk about including good memories of Copthorne and Shrewsbury and we all agreed that we'd had a good time and a complete change which had boosted our morale. At the Camp gate we shook hands and wished each other well, hoping we would see each other again soon. Something I found out from these lads was that as eighteen year olds who had recently joined the Regiment, we were to have a week's leave. Two lads had gone that week, so we were looking forward to our turn.

The following morning on parade, the emphasis was on self-preservation and survival if anyone of us became detached from the Regiment during a battle, as can happen in modern warfare. We had a lecture on the subject in the dining room until mid-day, which was given by two experienced officers whom I had not seen before. Lieutenant Gwilliam was also there and asked a lot of questions. After the lecture we found out that he was taking us on a sort of practical experience march on the next day and we were to stop out all night.

We were to leave Camp at 8.30am without breakfast and return the following day at 5pm.

When the whole Platoon were on parade at 8.30am next morning we were searched all over in case we had hidden some food, as we had to survive on what we could find out in the field. We were first taken by lorry about twenty miles to the more rough countryside and were dropped off down a lonely road. We were now on our own with Lieutenant Gwilliam who had a map, and he started us off down the road. After about an hour we turned into a wooded area where lots of pine trees were growing. We continued up a hill which was hard going because of large amounts of rocks. Eventually it was time to stop and settle in for the night. We had noticed an old Crofters' cottage nearby which was roofless but Lieutenant Gwilliam said we were to go to the cottage and see what we could do with it. The only things we had been allowed to take with us were our jack-knives, our cigarettes and matches as we would probably have these anyway if we were parted from the Regiment. "Now, time to get organised" said Lieutenant Gwilliam, "first we need some of you who have lived in the country to scout for food and we want a few of the strongest to volunteer to find wood or something to put some sort of roof on this cottage. We also want someone to get a fire going and the rest of you can clean out this tip so we can spend the night here." The old building had two rooms and a dilapidated toilet block. My old friend Taffy Evans and another Welsh lad and a Black-country man who had been farm hands were detailed to look for food. Josh Abrahams was to help organise and prepare a fire on the old remains of the stove, and four of the more hefty chaps were sent back to where the pine trees were to collect wood and branches etc. to make some sort of roof. One of the lads had already found an old cast iron pot under the rubble and an iron bar which was used to fix the pot over the stove. Everybody got going on their allotted jobs as there was not much time before dark. The floors of both old rooms were cleared of rubbish and we found stone floors underneath. The old fire stove was patched up with pieces of rock and Abrahams was busy picking up all the bits of dry wood to get a fire going. The three lads detailed to find food had disappeared looking for anything edible they could lay their hands on. Some of the old roof timbers were replaced across the corners of the walls and after a while we saw the boys coming back from the woods dragging a huge pile of branches up the slope so we went to give them a hand. After a couple of hours and a second load of branches, we had piled it over the roof timbers to make a roof. Whenever we were out in the wilds we always carried large rubber groundsheets to lie on and we decided to put these over the new roof and hold them in place with stones. There was bracken left over so we piled it on the floor as it would be better to lie on.

All this time, Abrahams and three others were going blue in the face blowing on the little pile of timber trying to get a flame. "Keep going men, there's smoke appearing now. You're doing great," remarked Lieutenant Gwilliam. Soon smoke was coming out of the old chimney and a small flame could be seen, and a big cheer came up from all around! It seemed that the secret of getting the fire going was that two or three of the lads who smoked had taken their cigarettes out of the boxes and had used the boxes to light the fire, which was soon properly burning after having choked most us with the smoke!

The three food hunters were still out and the light was starting to fade so Lieutenant Gwilliam detailed a couple of scouts to look for them. The mist was coming in when five figures were seen struggling along in the distance, so two more men were sent to help them. They were greeted with a cheer when they arrived. "What have you got there?" asked Lieutenant Gwilliam. "Two wild birds, a bag of swedes and some mushrooms." Another big cheer went up! "Get that bloody pot boiling!" called Taffy Evans – but in fact the pot had been on for a good half an hour, so that we could drink warm water if nothing else was available. The wild birds had been easily caught as they'd been found nesting in the bracken and after the men had killed two of them they'd gone off in search of mushrooms etc. They told us all this after the birds had been plucked and cut up into little pieces and put into the boiling water. About four good sized swedes were also cut up and put in the pot, followed by a pile of wild mushrooms that the lads assured us were O.K. to eat. We were all now in this battered old building with a roof that would only be O.K. if any rain that came was light. It must have been about eleven o'clock before Abrahams, who had been stirring the pot, eventually gave us the news that the food could be dished out. A mug was handed to Lieutenant Gwilliam who was going to see that we all got a fair share. I think I am safe to say we all had about two thirds of a mug each to everyone's delight. We sang 'Roll Out the Barrel' and had a jolly good laugh. Afterwards, Lieutenant Gwilliam thanked us – but it was he who kept up the morale. We than settled down, a bit cramped, on our bed of twigs and bracken from the woods.

About ten of us were detailed to divide the night up to keep a look out but most of us were awake by 6am. Some of us walked across to the small hillside stream and filled our water bottles ready for the march back to Camp. We then gathered around outside for Lieutenant Gwilliam to give instructions. "Right, men, I hope you are all feeling fit. There is no transport to pick us up but I have had a look at the map and I reckon we can save a few miles if we go across country to find the railway lines to Lockerbie. Now, all put your cigarettes out and let's go in single file." We all felt good but a bit weary after having slept huddled together. "Have you collected your ground sheets from the roof?" asked Lieutenant Gwilliam. "Yes" we replied. "Let's get moving then," he said, and off we went in single file.

Shortly after, the mist seemed to be clearing and the sun was popping through the clouds. We eventually came across the railway line from Dumfries to Lockerbie and followed that for a while then branched off towards Lockerbie as Lieutenant Gwilliam had planned, but before getting back to Camp we were in need of a rest. We came across a very large tree with branches spreading right out. "Halt men – we will rest under that tree. Refresh from your water bottles and smoke if you wish" we were told. The discussion was mainly about food and what the two birds were the lads had caught. It seemed they were grouse, and Taffy had crept up to them and clobbered them with a branch. The swedes we had were found in a pile by a gate leading to a small farm, so they picked up about a dozen. We brought the rest of these with us and we had cut them into quarters to eat on the way back. Our Platoon Sergeant told us of all the different berries and things we could eat including frogs etc. "I don't think Corporal Williams would ever starve, Sir" someone called out. "Is that right, Williams?" asked Lieutenant Gwilliam. At that, Corporal Williams found a snail in the grass and immediately popped it into his mouth and ate it to the disgust of everyone! "Well, I have seen everything now!" said Lieutenant Gwilliam, "but we will have to get on our way." We all got up and in single file started off on the last leg of our journey. We bypassed Lockerbie and entered the Camp from the back end at about 3.45pm and were immediately dismissed and we made our way back to our quarters. After about an hours rest we had a good wash and clean up and went over to the Mess where we had a laugh and a good meal then finally retired to our Huts for a rest and a natter. One thing we were all sure of – this new Officer of ours had won the respect of all the men and that was very important to us all.

Whatever I thought of others, this book is really all about my life. Yes, I found I could now cope with the conditions I may have to endure but that alone does not make a soldier and I wondered if that time would ever come.

I was having a good old moan at that time as I still had to face the test the next morning to see if I was capable of becoming a Radio Operator – an idea I loathed. "I'm going to make a right mess of the paperwork to get out of it" I commented. "You won't get away with it Boyo" said Taffy Evans. "I bet you I will" I replied, "I'll bet you five fags, Taffy." "O.K. you're on – five fags it is" he said. The Signals Officer was a Lieutenant Clapham who later was to become our Company Commander. He gave us each a paper with lots of questions, though some not relating to Signals. I made as many mistakes as I dared and thought 'that's it, they won't have me.' I knew I didn't shirk my duty but thought Signals etc. was not for me. I was going to try and get into the driving side if I could.

The next day we all had to go on a hand-grenade instruction course – though we knew about them but most of us had never actually used one, except the Regulars and a few Dunkirk lads. The British grenade is made of cast iron and breaks up into tiny fragments when exploding. It has a clip on the side which holds the detonator in place until it is released, but cannot be released until the pin is pulled out. The pin is fixed to a split ring like a key ring. We went in the back of a lorry with a box of live grenades and Lieutenant Gwilliam in charge. We arrived at a secluded piece of land where no harm could be done, and there was a large slit trench ready for the job. Lieutenant Gwilliam stood in the trench with the box of grenades and called out each name in turn and instructed us how to throw the grenades whilst the rest of us stood behind a large mound of earth for protection from the explosions.

About half the lads had their turn when my name was called. He handed me the grenade and went through the procedure of handling and throwing. I must admit he looked a bit stressed by that time, probably worrying in case one of us made a mistake. With the grenade gripped in my right hand, I inserted a finger of my left hand into the ring. "You have four seconds to duck safely after you have thrown it" said Lieutenant Gwilliam, "off you go." I pulled on the ring and it came off the pin, leaving the pin half way out – I saw him give me a look, but I pushed the pin back in with my thumb and reconnected the ring to the pin still gripping the lever and stopping it flying off. Without hanging about I pulled the ring and this time the pin came out properly and I threw the grenade and ducked as it exploded. Lieutenant Gwilliam looked relieved and said, "We shall have to stop now, Jones. We need to examine the rest of the grenades to see if the pins have been put in properly." Quite frankly I think he had had enough! When we got back it became a subject of discussion from a safety point of view.

At this point in the book I have to say that at the age I am now, it is difficult remembering names. I am finding that it is the nicknames that I can put a face to and there were so many of them. We had a few Taffys, a few Smudger Smiths and Nobby Clarks but there were a couple of specials. One chap was called Pancho; he had a bushy moustache, dark skin and dark hair and he claimed he had connections in Mexico. We never knew if he was telling the truth but he always insisted we call him Pancho. There was a Welsh chap who never minded being called Chang. He was short, stocky and very broad shouldered with a grin to match! He also had a slight bit of moustache either side of his broad mouth and had a beautiful set of pearly white teeth and when he smiled he did have the appearance of a Chinese man. He also had a deep baritone singing voice – but there is more to be said about this man later in the book.

A few days later I went into a depressive mood as I found out that I had actually been picked for the Radio course – after all I had done to get out of it! As expected when I went back to the Hut, Taffy said, "I told you so Boyo!" I called him a bloody spy and accused him of twitting on me, although I knew it wasn't true. "Come on, five fags you owe me" he said, so I threw them at him!

The course would be taken by Lieutenant Clapham and would be run in between normal training sessions rather than continuously which I considered not so bad.

It was now approaching the end of the year and a lot of training was being crammed in. Occasionally when we had to march some distance we did a forced march, which entails running 400 yards then marching 400 yards and repeating this for a long period. This is one thing that really tries men, especially when carrying a Bren gun or similar or if, like me, you're a bit of a short-arse!

I had now finished the Radio/Signals course which consisted of various means of using Morse Code by tapper, flag and lamp. It was never entered in my Pay book so I assumed I would not be wanted for the job – but the following year I found otherwise.

CHAPTER EIGHT

November 1943. Now the weather was making training much harder and I felt I could really do with a break, when out of the blue my name was on the notice board for a spot of leave. Another chap, Ted Smith, was also on the list for leave. He was a young chap who also came from Birmingham and joined up with me at Copthorne in Shrewsbury, which meant we were both travelling together to Birmingham, although he lived in Erdington a few miles from me. We had a total of eleven days – going on the Wednesday and coming back on Sunday of the second week. I immediately wrote home to let them know, as we still had about eight days before our leave. In the meantime another of the young chaps approached me and asked if I would do him a favour when I got home. He had a girlfriend who lived in Wolverhampton and he asked me if I could call and see her to give her a letter and a small parcel. I agreed to do this but did not know what I was letting myself in for. He then wrote to this girl and told her of the arrangement. The day soon came for our leave and we were dropped off at Lockerbie station where we boarded the train with not another soul on it. We couldn't wait for the train to get moving as we realized it was going to be a long journey and we were both so glad of this break. I'd had quite a few weekends off at Shrewsbury, but unknown to me at that time, we would all be getting more weekend leaves in the future, though not from Scotland. However of all the breaks, this one would be the most unusual and rather sad at times.

The train stopped at every station, picking up Service men and dropping some off which made it a slow journey home, but Ted and I enjoyed the great change. When we arrived in Crewe, everyone had to change trains. I was rather annoyed as the train we needed was already waiting on the platform and was packed full of people so we had to squeeze on anywhere we could and were separated. I didn't see Ted again until we were back in Crewe after our leave. It was 10½ hours from Lockerbie until, for some reason, I ended up at Snow Hill station instead of New Street, which meant I had further to walk. But I was glad to get off and stretch my legs.

As I was walking down Hill Street at about 12.30 in the morning, a young lady approached me and asked if I would like a couple of hours with her for a price. Well I had never had any sexual experience with any women and I was not going to start with her! "No thank you" was my immediate reply and I went on my way. When I got home the back door had been left open for me and a small bottle of beer was on the table with a note saying 'Welcome Home.' I went straight upstairs to bed and did not wake up until my mother woke me with a cup of tea at 10.45am the next day! After a good meal and I'd told my mother about my time in Scotland, I decided to go and see the girl I met when I was seventeen. I had seen her a few times but not for a long time but had written a few letters to her. At about five o'clock I knocked on the door of her house and her little brother came to the door. "Hello Robert, is Gladys in?" I asked. He looked a bit blank and said, "She's not here any more, she's gone away." At that, her mother came to the door and said, "Hello Ron, I'm sorry but Gladys met an American soldier and they got married and she's gone to live in the U.S.A. now." Well, that was that – what do I do now, I thought. I went straight home to gather my thoughts. "You're back early" Mother said. When I told her what had happened, she was very angry as she had seen and spoken to Gladys many times without any indication that she was seeing an American soldier. "Just forget it, Mom, we were never really serious and we were not engaged," I said. Then I told her about the prostitute who had stopped me when I was walking home from the train. "You want to be careful who you associate with these days," she warned. "Mom, I'm a soldier now and I'm old enough to look after myself, so stop worrying." But that was my mother, always worrying about us. I then told my mother that I was going over to Wolverhampton on the Sunday to see a girlfriend of one of the soldiers, to take her a letter and a small package. After a gasp of surprise from her, I fully explained the innocence of the visit and she understood.

On Saturday night my parents had arranged a 'Welcome Home' party, which was no surprise! Everyone came who was able to do so – my sisters and their boyfriends, a lot of my local friends and some neighbours. Everyone had something to eat and drink, and my mother as usual played a few tunes on the old piano and my Dad sang his amusing Army songs and we all joined in! There was never a dull moment when my parents threw a party for any of us.

On Sunday morning after a good breakfast and a few usual words of advice from my parents, I set off for Wolverhampton via train from New Street station. There was no problem getting a train there and I could use my Army pass I'd been issued with back at Camp. The porter made me sit in a Third Class coach as usual but gave me good directions where I had to go when I got off the train. The train arrived at about one o'clock and everywhere was very quiet being a Sunday. I had about a forty minute walk to the street where the girl lived. I quickly found her house which was very similar to the one where I was born in Birmingham. A middle-aged woman answered the door. "You are Ron, I believe" she said. "Yes, nice to meet you" I replied. "Pauline won't be a minute, she's gone to post a letter" I was told. Almost as soon as I sat down, she walked in. "Hello, you must be Ron" she said. I handed her the package and the letter, which she promptly put in a drawer. She thanked me very much and for some time we talked and she was interested to know how Leonard was and what he was doing, but I noticed that her mother was listening to everything we were saying and kept her eyes on us as though we were planning something, after all, Pauline was very attractive and seemed very forward. I was offered a cup of tea and a sandwich, but said I'd just have the tea. Whilst drinking the tea, Pauline's mother remarked, "We are going to the pictures this afternoon aren't we?" There was a strange look of surprise on Pauline's face and it was obvious that no arrangement had been made. I quickly said, "I haven't been to the cinema for ages – I'll come with you." So at about three o'clock we set off walking to the cinema and all the way Pauline's mother made sure she walked between us. I don't think it was me she distrusted, but her own daughter! On arrival she didn't offer to pay, so I forked out for all three of us, and when we found our seats, she sat between us – obviously mother knew best!

When we left the cinema it had started to get very foggy. In those days fogs were always very thick. Back at the house Pauline's mother made me a sandwich and a cup of coffee. Then Pauline asked, "Why don't you stay the night Ron, you can sleep on the settee?" I could see that her mother was surprised at the suggestion, so I immediately declined the offer. "Thank you very much for the offer, but I do have a lot of visiting to do tomorrow. My train is at ten-fifteen so I will have to leave here by nine-thirty." So we just continued to chat until then. When the time came for me to leave, I was shocked at how bad the fog was. I could not see the edge of the pavement! I quickly wished them both goodnight and made my way by asking people how to get to the station. I arrived dead on ten-fifteen but when I got onto the platform I could not even see the edge of it. I made my way to the Station Master's office – in fact he was the only one on the station. "Where are you off to, mate?" he asked. "Birmingham" I replied. "Well that train is running an hour late because of the fog" he said. I groped my way along the platform till I found a bench to sit on, and wrapped my overcoat around me and lit a cigarette. Whilst sitting there I calculated that if I walked at Army pace, I could be in my house for about one o'clock in the morning taking it that the train would go slowly. However, I did not expect what was to happen next.

I heard footsteps coming through the gate and on to the platform, and someone sat on the next bench but they were out of sight because of the intense fog. Then I heard this person crying quietly. I didn't want to get involved, but after a while I felt I had to investigate. I walked over to the bench and there was this very well-dressed young lady wiping her eyes. "Are you alright I asked. No reply at first. "Are you sure you're O.K." I asked again. Then in a quiet voice she said, "I have been sitting with my husband in the hospital all day, and he passed away this afternoon." My mother always told me to be careful of strange women, but this one seemed genuine. So I said to this young lady, "I'm really very sorry to hear that. Where have you got to get to?" "Birmingham" she told me. "I'm going to Birmingham too, I live there. Where about in Birmingham do you live?" I asked. "I come from Five Ways, by Broad Street" was the reply. "Well," I told her, "I know Five Ways very well as I used to be in the Home Guard at the Grammar School there." "Yes, I remember the Home Guard lads there" she said.

I sat down by her and said, "Look, it will be hard for you to get to Five Ways in this fog, would you mind if I escorted you all the way? The train is running late and I will make sure you get home safely I promise." I still couldn't see her face properly in the dark but it was obvious that she trusted me. "I would be very grateful if you did; my mother will be worried about me" she said. So I tried to get her talking. "My husband and I were in a band – I am a guitarist and he was a singer and piano player." She told me the name of the band that I had heard of, but cannot now remember.

It was about 11.20p.m. when I heard the train approaching. "Well we will soon be in Birmingham now" I said, but at that she cried uncontrollably. The train stopped and I had to help her on as she had a heavy bag of her husband's belongings. No-one else was in the coach and I could now see her face properly. I did not ask her but I reckon she was a little bit older than me, probably only two or three years, and very good looking but it was clear to me that she'd had a very stressful day at that hospital. The train pulled out and I suggested she should try and get some sleep. "If you like, as you have all of the seat to yourself, why don't you lie down. Give me your ticket and if you are asleep when the ticket collector comes, I will hand it to him." Without any question or hesitation she did exactly that, and was soon fast asleep. Ten minutes into the journey the ticket collector came in. "Is the young lady O.K.?" he asked, and I explained why she was spark out. "O.K. mate – take care" he said and off he went. I was longing to go to sleep myself but I did not want the two of us to end up past our stop. The train went very slowly all the way and it was about one o'clock when we pulled into New Street station. I was very careful of waking her up. She hadn't moved an inch since we had got onto the train. "We are in Birmingham" I said. She never answered, just sat there with a very bewildered look on her face. I took hold of her large bag and said, "Come on, you will soon be home." "My mother will be waiting up for me" she said. The fog here was not so bad and we had about one and a half miles to walk to her place, passing my own home. When we arrived at Five Ways, she said, "I live over there," and pointed to a large old Victorian house. By this time it was about 1.30am. I remembered the house – it had a long drive up to it. "I remember this house when I used to do Home Guard duty across the road" I told her. Immediately she pressed the bell the lights came on and her mother opened the door and they hugged each other tightly. "This soldier had stayed with me all the way home" the girl said. "Won't you come in and have a glass of sherry?" she asked. I thanked her for the offer but said no as I was very late now. I wished them both well and shook their hands and went on my way. I felt that was a sad encounter and over the years when I have been in that area of Five Ways I have often wondered what happened to them, as the old Victorian house is no longer there.

About eleven o'clock next morning I crawled out of bed and went downstairs. "You got home late last night" said my mother. Well I expected her to say that, so I explained everything to her. "That was very sad," she said, "what are you doing for the rest of today?" "Keep myself to myself and have a walk around Brum and the old Bull Ring" I replied, and that's exactly what I did. It brought back a lot of memories of when I was a child. On Sunday mornings there were all sorts of things going on; a preacher standing on a box and spreading the Gospel; a chap selling pills that would cure any ailment, (at least that's what he claimed), and an escapologist being tied up then escaping from his chains etc. – it was fascinating!

On the Tuesday I had a nice surprise. I bumped into my old school friend who went into the Navy two months before I was called up. I hadn't seen him for about nine months. He told me that he also had several days leave so we decided, as we hadn't seen each other for some time, we would make the most of it. "What about going to the Ice Rink in Spring Hill?" I suggested. "But I can't skate" said Dougie. "It won't matter" I replied, "we can have a laugh. The only thing is we will have to walk there and back as there are no trams running tonight." "Right, O.K. then, we will meet at 7.30 tonight at my house" said Dougie. This we did, but we did not expect the trouble it would cause us both.

The place was about two miles from where we lived, but as we were young and fit it was no bother to us. When we arrived, I showed Dougie where to get his skates. There were only about six youngsters on the ice. Dougie was struggling to get his skates on as he seemed very anxious to get on the ice before me. He gently went down the two steps onto the ice. "Be careful" I warned him, "hold onto the rail." But he insisted he was O.K. and he tried to walk further onto the ice; then suddenly he flipped over, giving his head a nasty bang. He lay there for a few seconds then tried to move but he had obviously really hurt himself. Two young girls came over and helped me to take him to the First Aid man who said, "I should take him to the hospital and get him checked out, as he does not look too good to me."

As there was no available ambulance there, I held him by the arm and we slowly walked back towards home and we eventually arrived at the bottom of the Bull Ring in Edgbaston Street where there was a Pub called the Wagon and Horses. As he felt a little better he said, "I could do with a drink." We stood in the passage, both with half a pint, but I could see that he was not at all right. "Come on" I said, "I'm taking you to the Queen's Accident Hospital." This was a place I had been to many times myself as a school boy, but it was still some way to go and difficult as I was now holding him up.

We arrived there about midnight and I managed to get him up the steps and through the main door. By this time he could hardly stand. When we got inside we were met by a large Nurse with an angry look on her face, and to our shock she said, "You can both get out of here – we have had enough of you lot tonight." Well, I was almost speechless. "What's the matter?" I asked. "My friend's been hurt." "You've been fighting in the Pub over the road" she replied. "No," I struggled to explain, "he's hurt his head at the Ice Rink." So she then fetched another nurse who helped Dougie inside and said angrily to me, "You sit there and wait while we look at him." I sat waiting for about half an hour and when the Nurse came back she asked, "Are you a relative?" "No, we are both on leave – we're friends." I told her. She explained that Dougie had to stay in hospital as he had concussion. She also told me that in the pub opposite there had been a fight between some Navy and Army chaps and she had thought we were some of them.

I then had to go to Dougie's mother's house to tell her the bad news, but they were all in bed. I threw stones at the bedroom window until his mother came to the window and shouted down, "What do you want?" "It's me, Ron, and I've to tell you that Dougie is in the Queen's Hospital with concussion" I told her. "Right, I'll get up and go to see him. Thank you Ron" she said. I went on home. I went to see Dougie a day or two later and he had recovered well. But it had ruined our little get-together. I didn't see him again until the war was over. The rest of the week I spent visiting friends and relatives and generally sight-seeing, but like all breaks they soon pass. I stayed at home all day Saturday to rest, as I had to go back to camp on the Sunday morning.

Both my parents and my eldest sister came to see me off. I stood in the coach shaking hands through the window, and all three wished me well but Mom did not look happy at all as she obviously did not want me to go. "I'll see you soon" I shouted as the train pulled out but when that would be no-one knew. The long ride back to Lockerbie was very slow as the train stopped at every station. The majority of the passengers were military personnel though no-one I knew to talk to. However I had a stroke of luck at Crewe where we all had to change trains; I bumped into Ted Smith who I'd lost contact with on the way down. We were so pleased to see each other as we would be company on our way back to Camp, and we had plenty to talk about regarding our leave – though occasionally we dozed off! It was about 10.15pm when we pulled into Lockerbie, and as usual there was no-one to pick us up, but it was no problem as after about half a mile walking in the dark we were given a lift by one of our lorries. We reported to the Guard Room at eleven o'clock and as we were both tired, it was a quick 'good night' and off to our quarters. I slipped my boots and tunic off, lay on the bunk and that was it – straight to sleep!

CHAPTER NINE

It was getting close to Christmas and the intense training seemed to by tapering off. It appeared that a few of the Officers and some of the men would be going home for Christmas as they had not had leave for twelve months. Some of our time was occupied with lectures to keep us on our toes. One of these was given by the Transport Officer. This lecture was of interest to me as I felt it was right up my street. The talk was all about the various vehicles and their general purposes, also the mechanics of them, which I had no difficulty in understanding. A number of times I was able to answer the questions we were asked and at one time the lecturer asked my name and Army number. I had always hoped I would eventually get on to driving but it didn't seem to be happening yet!

I was sitting on my bunk on the morning of Christmas Eve, when the Sergeant walked in and looked round at the men and when he looked at me he said, "Jones, come with me and bring your Army knife with you." I always thought that they picked on the small guys – at least that's how in seemed. So what was I to do this time? "Spud bashing" someone whispered as I followed the Sergeant. Outside were another four of the younger chaps. "Right, follow me" said the Sergeant, and he took us into a store room next to the Cook house and inside were three benches set into a triangle and in the middle was a huge pile of bloody spuds!! "Right you men, we need enough peeled for the whole Battalion for two days supply – now get cracking" he told us and off he went. "Have any of you done this before?" I asked. All the answers were 'no.' We had to keep peeling until the cook said there were enough and the peelings were thrown into the corner. The potatoes were very difficult to peel with an Army knife and I was beginning to wonder if the pile of peel was getting bigger than the pile of spuds as the peel was very thick! After a couple of hours the head cook walked in and he stared at the peel and then the spuds. "Blimey, I've never seen so many square spuds in my life; what have you been using, bloody choppers?" he asked, but with a smile. "O.K. that's enough. I'll get the pig farmer up the lane to collect the peel. He'll be pleased when he sees that lot." So that was us finished for the day.

Whilst we were together peeling the potatoes the four of us agreed to go into Dumfries after Christmas lunch even if we had to hitch-hike there. We reckoned it was about fourteen miles but could make it shorter if we went down some of the lanes. On Christmas morning we all greeted each other in a bit of Barrack-room fun. One or two were smoking cigars and some of the lads had made trimmings out of old newspapers and were putting these round the Hut. Breakfast was permitted half an hour later than usual and everything was done in good spirits. The dinner was a little more rowdy – lots of insults, though in a joking manner, about the cooks. They took it all in the Christmas spirit as they'd heard it all before! In general the dinner was good and well appreciated and the Officers kept a blind eye and deaf ear to all the remarks!

We four spud-bashers had other things on our minds though. Dumfries was our target for the night. After our lunch we prepared to go at four o'clock and set off as fast as we could, being certain we would pick up lifts, get in the pubs and come back by bus. We had previously seen buses with Lockerbie and Dumfries on the front. We walked the first mile then had a lift into Lockerbie. We then had a lift for a couple of miles with a farm truck and walked another three miles. Then an Army lorry picked us up and dropped us on the outskirts of Dumfries. To our horror when we got into the main streets, we could not find a bloody place open! "There's a bloke there" said Ted, "ask him." "Hey mate, can you tell us where we can find a pub?" we asked. "There's nay pubs open t'nach" he replied. "Are you saying that pubs don't open tonight?" "That's right the noo." We had properly dropped ourselves in it by not doing our homework! "What a load of pratts we are!" said Ted. "Well the best thing to do is to find the bus station and get back to Lockerbie – at least there is a fish shop there if we hurry," I suggested. "Hey mate, where's the bus station?" called Ted. "There's noo buses t'nach," was the reply. "Bloody hell, we're stranded and it's nine o'clock" said another lad. There was only one option now we agreed, and that was to get cracking back on foot. So we set off in the hope that we might pick up a lift. We were cursing each other and cursing Scotland as there was no-one about, after all it was a very lonely area. We passed through a little village which was deserted, not a soul in sight. In the square of the village was a statue of Robbie Burns, so out of spite we all stood round and peed up it!! We eventually arrived in Lockerbie at 2.30am. "Only another four and a half miles to go, lads" I said, and was answered with a few sarcastic remarks with a few swear words included. After we had walked a further mile, one of the lads said, "Listen, I think I can hear a vehicle coming." Sure enough he was right and an Army ambulance showed up. "Give us a lift, mate?" we asked. "O.K. hop in" the driver said. He dropped us right outside the gate and as we walked in it was 3.45am. "Had a good time?" asked the guard on duty. The answer was indescribable! That was a Christmas night we wanted to forget.

1944 started rather quietly but it was obvious things were about to happen. Early in the year the whole Battalion was being prepared to move but it was not until March that we realised that the moves for the Second Front were taking shape. The Russians had been waiting for the Second Front for some time. We in the 2nd K.S.L.I. had several moves in Scotland although I cannot be precise in which order they happened. These were to finally get the Battalion in shape for whatever we had to face. Early in 1944 the Battalion headed north to Nairnshire. We stopped a few miles from the town of Nairn and it was snowing all the time with ice underfoot. I thought it was the most desolate place in Scotland – the name Siberia comes to mind if I had to describe it. We were stationed on an airfield that was no longer in use. There was a row of accommodation huts on one side and about a quarter of a mile away was the Mess Hut which meant we had to walk in almost blizzard conditions to get our meals. I can remember the wind whistling under our tin hats. But why were we there? We could only think that it may be necessary for us to get used to the weather conditions if that is where the war was to take us. As we were to make such moves with speed, we could only think it was for the Officers and Battalion Commander to learn and get used to moving large numbers of men from one place to another quickly, which would be necessary in modern battle conditions. That was what some of us assumed, but the next move was more self-explanatory and told us a lot because of what we had to do. We ended up a little more south on the west of Scotland at a place called Gourock. I had never heard of it, but now will never forget it.

Gourock was a very pretty place surrounded by lots of waterways leading from the sea and up the Clyde where there were islands and lochs. The little town was like a little fishing village with white painted cottages right on the sea front and viewed from the sea it was really nice to look at. Our accommodation was good and we settled in quickly. After we had our first meal we were given a talk by the Commander who emphasised to us that whatever we did and whatever we saw was strictly top secret and none of us were to tell anyone else what we were doing. On that afternoon we were issued with 'Mae Wests.' These were inflatable life belts which the N.C.O.'s showed us how to use when we were back in our quarters.

The following day we were all taken in turn on a trip around the waterways on a Landing Craft. Was this what was going to happen to us? It appeared on the face of it that we were destined to attack somewhere by Landing Craft, but where would be the last thing we would get to know.

As there were several islands and lochs leading out to sea we had a number of different beaches or cliff landings to practice on. The first one chosen was a pebble beach – rather easy. The Craft came in slowly and we all stepped onto the beach making sure we got off in the right order and not knocking anyone over. Afterwards, we had a little discussion about it. A couple of days later, a rocky beach was chosen for a landing and we were to be dropped off in about two foot of water. There were plenty of rocks to climb over and a bit of an uphill slope to a grass plain on top. Our landing was again discussed the next day. I remember that we did not get into the boats to go back to the Camp, we always had to march there. The following afternoon we had to go to an area where it was very rocky and steep up to the top. A rope had to be fixed at the top so when we reached it we had to use the rope to haul ourselves up. This was very strenuous considering we carried all our equipment and also wore an inflated 'Mae West' plus a rifle. After the usual discussion it was decided that next time the lightest or fittest would go first to help the others to the top. When we tried again it did not seem any better – may be everything would be different under real war conditions.

A couple of days later a place was found with an overhanging cliff of about sixteen feet to the top from the water. It was also opposite an opening to the sea and the waves crashed against the cliff bottom so there was no way we could get off the Craft and stand at the base of the cliff. The plan was to drop a rope ladder down the cliff and secure it at the top, then each man in turn would stand on the front of the craft and as the incoming wave of water lifted the Craft, we had to grab the ladder and climb up. As the Craft slid back down with the wave, another man was to get into position ready for the sea water to lift the Craft again. The plan worked very well and was very fast, which was essential. Unfortunately the chap in front of me lost his nerve so was allowed to stay on the Craft. It turned out that on a previous training session some six months before, he was accidentally wounded whilst using live ammunition. He had survived a bullet going through his chest. Sadly he was now very nervous, as we could well understand. When ordered up the ladder he just cracked up and couldn't do it so he was allowed to stay in the Craft and go back to Camp. Presumably he was sent to a Base unit and stayed in England. Our practice carried on and was otherwise successful.

Our next and last landing was to be on a sandy beach. It's one I will never forget as I made a complete fool of myself. I was chosen to be part of a Bangalore Torpedo section. A Bangalore Torpedo is made up of three sections of cast iron pipe each six feet long, fitting into each other to make a tube of eighteen feet, and filled with explosive material. When the riflemen had cleared the beach, the Bangalore team would then push this length of pipe under the enemies' barbed wire defences. The last section of pipe had a detonator fitted which when set off had a four second delay, and the whole pipe would explode and blow a gap in the barbed wire so letting the infantry through. So the plan was set and the Craft loaded with men and equipment and off we went. We sailed out into the Clyde where a nice sandy bay had been found. The Craft was controlled by two Navy lads and we slowly headed towards the beach where we were to make the landing. I was sitting at the back with the third section of the pipe on my shoulder. As we neared the beach, one of the sailors started to check the depth of water as we were to be dropped in at about three feet. He kept throwing a weighted rope into the water and calling out the depth as we moved forward, 'sixteen feet; fourteen feet; twelve feet' and so on. I wanted to get a closer look at how he did this so I got off my seat and sat on the side of the Craft. When he shouted 'six feet' the boat lurched to one side as a wave hit it and with the weight of the pipe I lost my balance and over the side I went! With all the weight I had, my 'Mae West' just managed to keep my afloat. All I could hear was "Save your section!" which I'd let go. "Save your Bangalore section!" I kept hearing so I had to force myself under the water until I felt the pipe and grabbed hold of it. As soon as I surfaced they threw me a rope to hold on to and I clung on to the side of the Craft until I could walk on the bottom of the river and went ashore with the others. I was soaked from head to foot whilst the others were only wet up to their thighs. The Officers in charge were cursing in case the tube would not explode because of its soaking. However it was eventually pushed under the barbed wire defence and one of the Officers pulled the pin and disappeared fast! Luckily the pipe exploded and worked perfectly. We all charged through the gap and up the hill. Well, I'd made a mistake but one thing I did know – if I was in the real war I would never let that happen! We all marched back to Camp and were satisfied that it really went well after all.

February 1944. My nineteenth birthday on the 10th passed quietly with a letter and card from my parents, but there never seemed to be any celebrations for birthdays in the Army; too many things to do and think about in the Infantry.

The whole Battalion had been separated into smaller units and were in various training areas. Our Company had one more place to go to round it all up. We were taken to what was described as a Commando training outpost which was now vacant and we were to take the opportunity to use it for five or six days. We were transported to a small mountain Camp but as the narrow mountain road was icy it was too slippery for the laden vehicles so we had to jump out and walk. When we arrived all we saw were about three wooden army huts on the right and a couple on the left. One was the Cookhouse and one the Officers' quarters and they looked as if they had been there since before the war started. In charge was a Major who we had not seen before. He was soon nicknamed the 'Mad Major', and we had to do everything he wanted us to do. We were allotted our huts and then given some food and told we had to go on a march first thing after breakfast the next morning.

After breakfast, which was very sparse, we had to line up in front of the huts which were right on the edge of the road. We had no view to see as the whole area was covered in tall trees. We were fully dressed including tin hats, rifles and an empty pack on our backs. An N.C.O. came along and placed a large lump of rock in each of our back packs, and we then had to blow up our life jackets and put them on, which puzzled us because we knew there were no boats about. In single file we walked down the road which was still slippery with ice. The Mad Major was in front leading us and all we could hear was him calling out "keep going, men – keep going!" After we had been marching for about a mile, we turned down a path on the right through a wood and after a short distance we saw a loch with a concrete causeway leading into it. "Yes, keep going – into the water" the Major shouted. When the water reached our life jackets we had to turn round and walk back out. By this time snowflakes were falling and I cannot comment on what was said by the men! "Right, men, in single file at the double, back to the Camp" called the Major. We arrived back wet and cold. The only heating we had was an old cast iron stove in the middle of the Hut and it was constantly stoked up until it glowed red as we had an abundance of coke. We all sat as near to it as possible, sitting in our underpants and drying out our trousers and socks. No-one seemed to be grumbling as we had been through that kind of situation before. After a good meal we all slept well.

The following morning, breakfast was not allowed. We were put into groups of six with an N.C.O. Each group was given a map with three points marked on it. At these points were Officers who were to give us a ticket to prove that we'd reached the places in the right order. At the third point was a truck with a hot meal waiting for us. We had to take our utensils and mugs in our packs. Each group set off at ten minute intervals. There were no villages or buildings or roads to navigate by, only hill contours and streams of which there were plenty. The planners of the operation also made sure that whatever route we took we would all have to wade through a mountain stream. Our little group eventually arrived at the food truck at about four thirty in the afternoon and we could not get our mess-tins and mugs filled quickly enough! Two of the groups did get lost and never arrived at the food wagon, so a search party with torches was sent out in the dark. They were finally found and arrived very late, to enjoy a good hot meal. By this time the rest of us were in our Huts drying out, smoking and singing all sorts of songs.

The next day we only had to do some forced marching, once we were down on the flat road, and we marched for a couple of hours then returned to Camp. The day after, we did very little which pleased us – and we learned that the Mad Major had to return to his Regiment so had called a halt to our activities. The day after, we were relieved to see our transport arrive and after tidying up the Camp we were taken back to our Base Camp. It was very quiet and peaceful back at the old Camp but there was an air of anticipation with the men, all thinking of what the next few months were going to bring. I felt better than I did when I first joined the Regiment. Then, the men were all older than me with lots of Army experience which made me feel detached from them, but things were much different and I felt part of it all after all the training etc. we had been through. There was a quiet sense of comradeship and we all got on together and that is really what is required when we were going into the war together. I also have to say that the Officers had a wonderful understanding of the men and that gave a great feeling of confidence now that our training was finished and we were ready to do whatever was intended.

It was now mid-March and things seemed to be on the move – lots of meetings between the Officers and Commanders were taking place. We were given orders to pack our kit bags ready to travel and these were loaded onto the vehicles. We had to make sure nothing was left behind. All the stores were put onto trucks and one was loaded with weapons and ammunition. Then the troop carrying trucks arrived to take us to the railway station and once on the train we were not allowed off until we reached our destination so that no-one could find out where we were going.

CHAPTER TEN

After the train arrived at the station it took about twenty five minutes for us all to embark. This time we had coaches with corridors; when going on leave they were the old type with no corridors, but fortunately I knew all the lads in the coach I was in. I had not even noticed that the train had slowly pulled out of the station and it seemed a sad and bewildering moment after all the experiences we had shared in the area.

As the train sped away we all got chatting. "I wonder where fate will take us" said one of the lads. "We never know our fate" someone remarked. "Perhaps they will dump us in the middle of Wales where Taffy over there lives!" said another. "Not on your life, Boyo; we wouldn't allow you lot there – we would have to lock up all the women!" replied Taffy. "I wonder what the German Frauleins are like" said Ted Smith. "You've got to get there first," said the Sergeant. "Shut up and get your heads down, we have a long journey ahead." From somewhere down the corridor, we could hear Chang singing in his deep baritone voice – the trouble was that he was singing in Welsh so in our coach only Taffy knew what the hell he was singing about!

We were now officially on our way. I put my head back to try to sleep but in the back of my mind I was reminiscing about all we had done and realising things about myself. I had done everything that the others had and although I was now nineteen years old I still looked young for my age and I knew that I was an emotional person so I wondered how I would cope with whatever I had to do.

As usual the train stopped many times and we still didn't know where on earth we were going. After about three hours we stopped while some boxes of sandwiches and tea where loaded on to the train for us. This had obviously been pre-arranged, but again we were not allowed off the train for security reasons. Eventually we arrived at Hayward's Heath station, where our transport was waiting. After lining up and stretching our legs we were given a mild lecture by the Commanding Officer. "On our way we will be passing through the small town of Hayward's Heath, rather a reserved type of town. We want you men to be on your best behaviour as a true soldier should be." I think that was like asking a caged up lion not to bite anyone if it got out! However, as we passed through the main street there were a few cat-calls and whistles but nothing serious. Eventually we branched off the main road and into a wooded encampment of tents and military vehicles. We disembarked and were allotted to various bell-tents which were to be our home for the next three months – still not knowing where we were going. After we had been shown where the Mess tent was, the First Aid post, toilets and everything else, we soon settled in – especially as the weather was perfect and warm.

A couple of days later we went out on a keep-fit run outside the area of the Camp, and it quite frankly opened our eyes. None of us had seen such a massive build up of military equipment in all our Army service. Even some of the private dwellings had been commandeered for military use. There were tanks, trucks and all kinds of Army vehicles parked in private gardens with row after row of artillery and anti-tank guns etc. There wasn't a square yard of vacant space anywhere and this was obviously the result of long careful planning by very dedicated people, people who realised the need for secrecy and commitment to make sure the plan, whatever was going to take place, did not fail. I think by this activity we all knew roughly what was to happen soon – only at this stage we did not know where and they made certain, for a while anyway, that we were not to know. That is why we were constantly reminded of the need for all of us to remain silent about what we had seen.

We were all quite happy on the Camp; the billets were comfortable, the food was pretty good and we were not suffering from the bitter cold as we had been in Scotland. The following week we had a nice surprise. We were given the O.K. to go home on weekend leaves and we would be given weekend passes from Fridays after lunch and make our own way home via the railway. So half of the Company could apply one week and the other half apply for the following week. Ted Smith and I applied straight away and had the O.K. for that weekend. The rest of the week we sorted out the best plan, that being to get a lift into Brighton, take a train to Euston station in London and from there on to Birmingham. Ted would have to get off just before Brum as he lived on the opposite side of the town to me. We even found the times of the trains and if we made the connections, we would be in Brum on Friday evening. After lunch on Friday we applied for our passes; in fact there were six of us going to Birmingham. The obvious route would be to get a lift to Brighton which was only about eight miles away, catch a train to London then from Euston station to the Midlands. Just before we booked out we were joined by about another eight lads from another Company who had arranged a lift in one of our trucks which was going to London, and the driver was prepared to take them to Euston station, so after a quiet chat with the driver he said he'd take all of us if we were prepared to wait half an hour. This was all arranged and off we went. We were all cheerful and jubilant, especially when we boarded the train at Euston.

These weekend leaves became more regular and enjoyable; we almost forgot what we were there for at times, but were always reminded of the importance of saying nothing about what we knew. Whenever I met my family I never said a word about it, only that we were now stationed down south in a nice Camp. Many times we had to thumb a lift and go via Brighton but it was always great by whatever means. The weather was great, and in between our leaves we had to keep fit with various walks, marches and exercises. The whole of April was marvellous weather, but at the end of the month when we applied for our passes, we were reminded that these were to be the last ones. Each time I went on these little leaves I always said, "I will see you, Mom, in two weeks," but what was I to say this time? – I would have to tell her a lie.

Whilst at home I kept things as normal as possible, but on late Sunday afternoon I started to get ready to go back to Camp. My mother and father were in the house and also my eldest sister with her husband, who was a Sergeant in the Army Service Corps. I shook hands with him and casually remarked to my mother, "I won't be coming home for a few weeks as we are changing Camps so we will be busy." She had a disbelieving look on her face, so I hurried out of the house with my kit and walked quickly down the street. I had only gone about a hundred and fifty yards when I heard my mother calling me, but I pretended not to hear her and carried on without turning back. This was my mother all over, she knew I was lying to her.

Years later my sister reminded me of this incident and said my mother went back into the house and cried, knowing something else was about to happen. I met some of the other lads at New Street station and it seemed they had similar problems with their families.

It was the beginning of May. The build up was getting intense and masses of boats and ships filled the harbours. During the latter end of the second week I had a great disappointment. A Sergeant whom I did not know, walked into the tent and in a rather tense voice said, "Jones, follow me." I thought I had done something wrong as he seemed to be up tight. I followed him to the Stores whereupon he pointed to a box on the floor and snapped, "Right, that's yours." (I think he must have had some sort of telling off). "What is it?" I asked. "You are now our Company Radio Man" he said. I opened the box and in it was a radio transmitter that was totally strange to me. "But I've had no training with that type of radio" I remarked. "You're our Radio Man now" he said again, and off he went. I was quite upset at this as nothing was ever put in my Pay Book which is usually the practice if you were a qualified Radio Operator. I also thought of the importance of giving me a radio receiver to use considering the seriousness of what we were about to do and I did not know any of the laid-out communication codes for whatever the plan was. I felt that he had put me in a very difficult situation. I complained to my own Platoon Sergeant and he was also rather concerned. "Just a minute," he said, "I may be able to get you some help." He thought for a while then said, "Come with me and bring the radio." He took me to another Company who had a Radio Operator with the same type of radio and explained the problem. I knew this other chap as I had been on a course with him nine months before. "Bloody stupid to have that dropped on you at a time like this! But don't worry, you know all the basic procedures – I'll help you out." After a bit of instruction I got the hang of it, then he wrote down all the call signs for all the Companies including the Support Company and the Head Quarters, which I quickly memorised then destroyed the paper. "O.K." he said, "when you get back, give me a call; I will respond, then do it a couple more times tomorrow and that should be fine." I thanked him for his help and felt happier and within a few days I was more confident. The only thing that did worry me was not knowing what to do in an emergency, but I was feeling better about things in general. I never found out what had really happened but it was suggested that the previous Operator had gone sick.

In the last week in May all the N.C.O.'s and Radio Operators were called upon to go to a very large tent which was being used as a Briefing Room. I had never been in there before. It really was an eye-opener – inside was a massive model of a section of Normandy Beach, code named 'Sword.' Every building, every street was made in miniature; it was perfect. All the road numbers were there which we had to remember and all the places and the assembly areas were shown. Right at the top was the town of Caen, which after a lot of briefing we were told was to be the target. The name of the whole operation was coded 'Overlord' and all the small villages also had code names. So now we knew we were to make a major assault on the coast of Normandy which must not fail. Now I knew why all the training in Scotland had been done at speed – this was essential we were told, by the Officer instructing us, not to give the enemy any chance to stop us. The element of surprise was very important as the enemy was to be fooled into thinking the landings were to be at the narrowest part of the channel at Pas de Calais. The R.A.F. was to drop millions of tiny pieces of copper strips over there to block the Germans' Radar and fool them into thinking thousands of planes were going over, and they probably believed we would not attempt to cross the channel at the widest part (about 100 miles), which is exactly what was planned. Eventually every man was to visit this Briefing Room to see the extent of what had been done and what was expected. It was a brilliant piece of planning with no stone left unturned.

We were then briefed regarding the plan of action. The 6th Airborne were to land at midnight in their Gliders and capture the bridge over the River Orne, which would be on our Battalion's left flank, so that the enemy could not cut us off from getting to Caen. There would be three Battalions in No. 8 Brigade to land before us to secure the Bridgehead. Then 185 Brigade comprising the Royal Norfolk's in reserve would land. The 2nd K.S.L.I. would press forward as hard as they could up the D.60

road with the Royal Warwickshire Regiment on our right flank. First we would have to negotiate through Lion-sur-Mer, past the village of Hermanville, through Beoville, through Bieville to take Lebisey then Caen. That was the plan. To the northern edge of Caen would be about ten miles from the beach. The planned date was the 5th of June – 'D-Day' – providing the weather stayed as it was expected.

The mood amongst the men remained cheerful and as it was now the last week in May most activities were the re-checking of equipment and weaponry. We were not aware of it at the time, but it had been estimated that along the whole of the invasion beaches 20,000 casualties could be expected in the first 24 hours.

The next plan was that we embark on the Landing Craft in the early afternoon of the 4th June. All the Craft would go out to sea then line up and get into the planned invasion order before midnight, ready for the morning of the 5th June. The planning for this must have been an enormous task but we were now ready and we all had the full equipment we were to land with. In my own case I would have my rifle with 100 rounds of bullets, two hand-grenades, two spare Bren gun magazines, one pressure-type of land-mine clipped to my belt, a full water bottle, emergency rations and the radio. We all hoped we would be dropped off in very shallow water.

On the morning of the 4th June, after a good breakfast, we got ready and marched to the quayside of New Haven, where the amount of men and equipment was staggering. In single file, like everyone else, we climbed up the ramps of the Craft. After we had been aboard a couple of hours, we were ordered off again! It appeared that the weather at Normandy had deteriorated so the Operation had been postponed for safety reasons. This was a bitter disappointment to all especially the Officers who had done so much to get the organisation correct. Now it was to be done all over again. We returned to our Camp and just waited for further information. After a few hours sleep we were told that as the weather had improved, the Operation would be taking place that night, 6th June, as had previously been planned. We once again boarded the Landing Craft in single file. It felt very cramped but no-one was saying much at all.

Towards evening the Assault Craft started to move slowly out to sea along with all the rest of the fleet. We had to go out quite a long way as there were so many Craft etc. The whole armada had to spread out into the right order before the attack could take place but we were steadily approaching Normandy. Most of us were trying to snatch some sleep in our cramped situation and in doing so had not realised how quickly the night had gone. We could now hear the bombardment by the Navy on the German defences – it was one continuous noise.

"Get your equipment on!" called the Platoon Sergeant. We were obviously very close, but on an L.C.I. (Landing Craft Infantry) not everyone could see what was happening due to the high sides. With about a mile to go most of us now had a full view; it seemed the whole coast was erupting. Sometimes the enemy would bombard the area with mortars. They had fixed metal defences below the water line so the ships and Landing Craft had to ram the beach and risk damage to the boats. We could now hear the crunching of metal below our Craft, which came to a halt and we then waded off the ramps into about 1½ foot of water. We saw a few bodies floating in the water and some on the beach; they had done their job. In single file we hurried to the allotted assembly area ready for the advance. Within about 15 minutes the whole of the four Companies, W, X, Y, and Z, were accounted for and ready to move. When we had located the D.60 road to Caen, X Company was to advance on the left of the road followed by Y Company and W Company on the right of the road followed by Z Company, but first we had to get to the south side of Lion. Judging by the model we were shown back in England, it would be no problem to find.

First we had to turn right past a row of private houses and as we did so the people came out and stood on their doorsteps to talk to us, but we had to move fast and signed to them to go back indoors which they did. We were soon through Lion and on to the road we wanted. We could then see the real danger as the road swept out into open country and the Germans had the advantage of having the high ground right in front of us. The original plan was for the K.S.L.I. to wait for the tanks to come up and while mounted on them we could attack and advance more quickly. The idea was soon dropped as we could not wait for enough tanks to get off the beaches and get to us in time. So it was decided to advance on foot. Then we experienced our first terrible sight as one of the soldiers up at the front was blown to pieces, either by a mortar shell or perhaps the land-mine he was carrying may have been hit by a bullet as we were now in full view to the enemies' advantage.

The Royal Warwickshires were now on our right flank and also advancing in the open countryside. Two of our tanks, about 300 yards to our right, had been spotted by the enemy and were having a rough time and one had received a direct hit from the anti-tank guns on the high ground. At that, Lieutenant Gwilliam came and asked me to report our position to the Head Quarters, after he had given me the map reference. This I did with no problem. "Did you get a reply?" he asked. "Yes sir; they just said congratulations and keep going." To my surprise he thanked me for taking over the position of Company Radio man. It was obvious he was not aware of how I got it!

We had now passed the crossroads near Hermonville. To the west was the Royal Warwickshire Regiment; to the left, or east, was the River Orne. We had been informed that the 6th Airborne Troops had captured the bridge over the River Orne at Benourville.

It was known at the start that the 21st Panzer Division was somewhere in the area of Caen, or to the east of the River Orne, so with the bridge captured they would have to go round Caen to the south before they could get to us. We were already moving as fast as possible and could not afford any hold-up if we were to get to Caen. As we advanced over open country, still following the D.60, we were closing in on Beauville and were receiving quite a bit of attention with gun fire. Then from our right flank we spotted some armoured vehicles coming from the high ground. It was obvious they did not realise how far we had advanced. Our Support Company knocked out two of these vehicles from the rear. In the village itself we encountered a lot of opposition but our Forward Companies were dealing with them although it cost us some wounded including an Officer. We eventually took the village by skirting round the east and west and from the front with all four Companies.

To get to our objective, once more we had to move swiftly. We next had to take Bieville. After that the ground was more uphill to Lebisey Wood and Caen was hidden from view as after the high ground the road dipped down again into Caen. Before we reached Bieville we were surprised to see on our left, some of the Gliders that had landed in the early hours of the morning and we were greeted by some of the Airborne Troops as we continued our advance. The opposition was getting more intense and we had to negotiate our way very carefully as the Germans must have been well aware of the situation by now. Y Company was pushing forward into front position under Major Steel. Some civilians had come out of their houses to see what was happening and obviously did not realise the danger, so were warned to keep inside. Most of the gun fire was still coming from the high ground on our right, but very difficult to observe owing to the terrain; all we could do was to hope that our mortars from Support Company and our light artillery would keep them occupied. The R.A.F. had pounded all those gun positions early in the morning but it could not be expected that they had all been knocked out.

When eventually we occupied Bieville the road in front was very narrow but started to go up steeply to Lebisey Wood which ran right across the top of the hill and obscured our view, though not the enemies view. Occasionally we got a few bursts of machine gun fire and we could detect the bullets striking the trees around us. Then for quite some time we stopped advancing, and we heard the bad news that our Company Commander Major Steel had been badly wounded. It was some time later that worse news came that he had died.

Soon after we had to move forward again up the steep narrow road. The banks either side were high with a hedge on top. The enemy obviously knew where we were but could not see us. The problem was we did not know and could not see them. As we moved further up the road we came across the most awful sight. There were three German soldiers, or should I say the remains of them, on the road surface. They had obviously been crushed under the tracks of retreating enemy tanks. Only one of them had the top half of his torso with his head and arms untouched. These things bring the real horror of war home to you, just as we had seen that British soldier blown apart at Hermonville when we had to step over his body parts. We seemed to be static now for some time, but all I wanted to do was to get away from these awful scenes.

The Platoon Sergeant came down from a little way up the road. "Jones, Lieutenant Gwilliam wants you up there straight away" he said. As I walked up the hill, most of the men were leaning against the banks looking very tired – after all some of them had not had proper sleep for forty eight hours. "Right Jones," said Lieutenant Gwilliam, "I need to report the situation after I have assessed it. I am going up the bank and through the hedge to see the exact situation – now follow me." I followed him a further fifteen yards up the hill and then we had to climb the bank and get through a small gap in the hedge. From there we crawled on our hands and knees up the grassy slope. We spotted a large cast-iron cattle drinking trough right on the edge of the wood. "That will be ideal" he said, and the two of us then lay flat so as not to be seen. Lieutenant Gwilliam then searched the area using his field-glasses. Far over to the right of the wood he spotted a group of German soldiers. "I think there are about thirty and they look as though they are digging in" he remarked. "Now get in touch with Support Company and I will give you the map reference. Ask for help with some mortar fire onto that map reference." This I did and they agreed to comply. We waited about five or six minutes then we heard the sound of four shots from the 4" mortars. We waited a few seconds then heard the sound of them coming over. They all exploded in the vicinity of the enemy and they seemed to disappear. Then Lieutenant Gwilliam said something to me which must have been the worst decision of his life. "Just wait here, Jones – I'm going to have a further look directly in front of us." In a stooped position he went into the wood holding his revolver. He must have only taken three paces when he was badly wounded from a burst of bullets. The Platoon Sergeant in the meantime had moved up level with us but still on the road. "What's happened?" he shouted. As soon as he knew, he called the stretcher bearers up. Lieutenant Gwilliam had to be dragged back behind the cattle trough and we removed all his equipment and placed him on the stretcher. His face was white with pain. They slid him down the bank – and I never saw him again. With the loss of two of our valuable Officers and the time getting on, we waited for further orders which soon came. We were to move back down the road and form a defensive position on the edge of Bieville.

When we arrived back at Bieville, some of the men were detailed to dig two-man trenches around the front of the village, but the light had gone making it very difficult. The rest of the men were trying to snatch a bit of sleep in a cottage by the side of the road. This cottage had a cellar which allowed men to get some sleep. When the trenches had been dug we all had to take a turn to be on look-out through the night. We did not get into Caen, but I do not think that any Commander could be dissatisfied with what the Regiment had achieved. We had come nine miles from the beach and met opposition all the way. Two of our Officers had been killed, four wounded and a further 107 other ranks killed or wounded – a total of 113 lost. I don't think I would ever be called a hero – I was bloody scared all the way from Hermonville and Bieville after seeing those awful sights. D-Day was over but the worst was yet to come. The casualties were light in comparison to what was estimated and I'd hoped it was always to be like that.

CHAPTER ELEVEN

During the next couple of weeks a lot of defensive work was being done to gather information about the enemy, through patrols by day and night. We had been shelled quite often but we always gave them more in return which kept their heads down. The British Infantry had a motto about defending, i.e. 'The best method of defence is to attack' in other words – keep the enemy occupied. The Royal Warwickshire Regiment attacked the Germans on our right flank and in turn so did the Royal Norfolk Regiment, but in both cases our attacks were repulsed.

Over on the west side of Caen was Carpiquet Airport. The Canadian Third Division was well over to our right and had several attempts to capture the airfield so that it could be used by our own Fighters and after a hard struggle the Canadians did eventually take it.

With the Germans still holding the high ground, any attack by the British was made all the more dangerous for that reason. The Germans also had a weapon that was extremely dangerous to advancing Infantry. It was the German Nebelwerfer. This weapon was a six barrelled Mortar gun that fired 5½" shells and when fired each barrel would be fired very quickly, but individually, and when the shells came down they would make a screeching noise so the British named them 'Moaning Minis.' They were very accurate and all the shells would drop in a cluster. These were far superior to our own 4" Mortars – but the German 5½" Mortars were easily recognised by the noise they made.

Chang, the Welsh soldier we had in our Company, proved to be a very useful and brave man. It was necessary for us to try to find out which German Regiments we had in front of us. Chang was a bit of a loner at times; he liked to do things by himself. He did not like going out on patrol with a group – he was quite happy to do it alone. He would set off after dark and disappear somewhere into the German lines and re-appear in the early hours. He always came back with evidence of the German Units. Many times he came back with soldiers' Pay-books. Sometimes he would have a German tunic or part of one with all the identification badges on them. No-one would ever ask him how he acquired them, but knowing Chang we could only guess. Chang was given the Military Medal for his actions. When we went to the Front again, he continued to do what he had started. One morning he brought back a prisoner. Sadly he went out one night and never returned, only to be found when the Regiment advanced some weeks later. Chang had been caught and shot. He died a hero.

I did four patrols, but not on my own; two night patrols and two daylight patrols. Two of these were very scary. In the first patrol we were a group of eight with a Platoon Sergeant in charge. It was a daylight patrol over to our left flank near and along part of the Orne canal. It had been suspected that the Germans had infiltrated into this area and we needed to find out, so we were well armed in case of contact with them. We came across some factories and work shops, but all deserted though we did find evidence of German soldiers having been there some time before. We found empty enemy cartridge shells inside a brick building and it was obvious they had been firing from the window. There were also some empty food tins. There was nothing else to do there so we went back and reported our findings.

The next time was very unusual, and lucky for us. Again, I cannot be exact but I believe there were nine of us including a Platoon Sergeant. We left after dark and had been given a small fluorescent yellow sheet of cloth to hang on the front of our tunics when we returned. This was to prove who we were when returning to our own lines. Off we went, the Sergeant in charge having had his instructions. The whole idea was that as the attack would have to begin again soon to capture Caen, we would have to push forward so every bit of information was required for it to be a success. Although it was about 11pm it was reasonably clear as the moonlight was coming through the gaps in the cloud and we picked our way round a partly wooded area. To me it seemed we were going round in a half circle and it was obvious something was wrong. Suddenly we had a shock as a German soldier, without warning, popped up out of a dug-out in front of us. Luckily for us he was facing the opposite direction. He stretched out his arms and yawned out loud. The Sergeant said "Heil Hitler" and the soldier in surprise spun round and the Sergeant shot him. No sooner had that happened when two other soldiers appeared with their backs to us, from a dug-out about twenty feet to our left. We all shot at them and they both went down where they stood. It was now obvious we were behind their row of trenches – German voices could be heard. "Let's get out of here, quick" we heard the Sergeant say in a quiet voice. Those of us with automatic weapons raked the area with gun fire then sped off as fast as we could, this time in the right direction. There were some shots fired at us but it was all very confusing. We thought that the Germans were as shocked as we were and were confused where the firing was coming from. When we got back the Sergeant reported what had happened, and nobody, including us, could hardly believe our luck – plus the fact we now knew approximately where some of their trenches were.

The next patrol I went on was easy to remember as the date was July 6th exactly one month after D-Day. Nothing much happened on the actual patrol – hardly anything to report as little or nothing was found, but even this was never reported after what happened just as we arrived back. Our Front line trenches were deep and partly covered; about 25 feet behind were our two-man dug-outs. As we passed the Sentry he said, "Hurry up lads, the cocoa is being dished out." Two of us nipped into the little dug-out; the other chap had only been with us a few days as a replacement. As we sipped our cocoa I recognised the sound of a large aircraft, obviously a bomber, very high up. It was travelling north towards the channel. Then I heard the very distinctive sound of a bomb coming down. Living in Birmingham during the Blitz, I was used to the noise. "Duck down!" I shouted to the new chap, "this bomb is going to drop very close to us – get right down!" I repeated. A few seconds passed then a dull thud and almost immediately large lumps of earth fell on us. I looked out of the trench and saw a massive crater with the edge of it only about eight feet from our dug-out. "It didn't explode!" exclaimed the new chap. "But it did," I said, "the blast has gone right over our heads by a couple of feet and when that happens you won't hear the explosion." Sadly the bomb had dropped within feet of our Front line trench – four men were killed while sleeping and the look-out man was seriously hurt with both legs broken. They all had to be dug out in the morning. That's another patrol I will never forget. It was a night where another five men were lost and our front line trench destroyed.

The day after, we received some more very bad news. Lieutenant Colonel F.J. Maurice, our Battalion Commander had been killed by shell fire. This was a terrible blow as the Brigade was gearing up to take Caen and the surrounding ground.

I cannot recall the exact date the assault took place or any of the fine details of the plan. What I do remember is that on the 7th or 8th of July we were ready to attack. We all watched as the Bombers went in and had a perfect view as all the bombs went down like strings of beads. The sky was perfectly clear and we felt that the Air Crews would have no problem knocking out the defences. After a while tons of dust appeared everywhere even showering down on the waiting troops. We were all encouraged by this bombardment.

Early the following morning, about 4am on the 8th July, our Artillery bombardment started. I remember we began to advance about twenty minutes after the barrage started. It was an uphill attack as the German defences had held the high ground for some time. It seemed to be about mid-day when we had reached somewhere near the top. The German gunners were still holding their positions judging by the considerable gun fire coming from them and it cost our Regiment quite a few casualties. The weather was getting very hot. Caen was down below the level of the top of the hill and we were able to see the remains of some of the higher buildings. As we continued to advance we were under attack from the German multi-barrelled Mortars, or 'Moaning Minis' as we called them. There was an N.C.O. on one side of me and I believe on my right was a private of the platoon, when a half-track vehicle came up and stopped just to the right of us. I believe it was an Artillery spotter vehicle with a crew of four, for sending directions to the gunners. Almost as soon as it had stopped a salvo of 'Moaning Minis' were heard coming in our direction and it was obvious to us three that they were going to land right where we were. "Take cover!" shouted the N.C.O. and all three of us dived under the vehicle. We heard all five shells drop and explode a few feet away. "O.K.

My Mother.

My Father on his arrival in France.

The 2nd wave landings, June 6th.

Carriers of the support companys moving in, June 6th.

The first of many.

Pressing on inland, June 6th.

The Regiment moving towards Caen on D60 RD, June 6th.

The day after Caen was captured. I saw this picture taken.

Left: Servicing the Carrier.
Right: In Ramallah Barracks Palestine late 1945, M.T. Section.

Myself brewing up on patrol in the desert.

The lads taking a break on patrol.

The Regiment leaving Palestine, 1946.

Me and Joan near Pegasus Bridge France.

Left: Myself. Photograph taken on my 21st Birthday in Jerusalem, 1946.
Right: Joan and family in first house.

let's go" he said sharply. "Hang on – there's a bloody tank coming out of the wood!" I shouted, but too late – it hit us with a high explosive shell and I was deaf for a few seconds. The first thing I saw was one of the crew jumping about with his trousers on fire. I got myself out from under the vehicle and clouted the soldier's trousers attempting to put the flames out. He had not realised that he also had an injury just below his ear. After undoing his personal First Aid kit, I gave him a dressing and told him to just hold it on and then get out of the way. As he was very dazed I pointed him in the right direction and told him to go. A quick look inside the vehicle told me the other three had no hope. By this time the others had crawled out from under the vehicle. One had a damaged arm and the other had shrapnel injuries to his legs and back. The Medics were close by so they had immediate attention. After gathering my senses, I went back under the vehicle to retrieve my radio and my rifle, but the rifle was damaged beyond repair – the wooden stock ripped off by shrapnel; the radio was also damaged. I was the only one not to receive an injury. I noticed the tank which had attacked us was going backwards and on fire. That was probably the nearest escape I had experienced up till then. I felt I may not be so lucky next time.

We moved forward as the day went on until the Germans had given up at that stage. Some of our men moved into abandoned enemy trenches. I recognised one chap, a Corporal Brown. By this time the weather was humid and the day had made us sweat so much. I jumped into the trench with them. "Here you are, Jonah, have a drink of this" said Brown. In the trench was a quantity of bottles of wine, some unopened and left by the Germans. I had never drunk wine before in my life. Where I lived in the back streets of Birmingham, to us it was a drink for the rich. I quickly drank about a third of a bottle, and very soon I felt my legs go weak and I slumped into the corner and fell fast asleep!

Caen was now almost in full view but we were not completely prepared for what we were about to witness as we walked in. The devastation was unbelievable. We were looking to see if anything at all had survived destruction. As we moved in we came across a church which seemed to be the only construction that was not completely destroyed. A few of us climbed up the steps leading into the church and we all sat there for a while with our thoughts. "It looks like we did not just capture this place – we completely destroyed it as well" remarked Corporal Brown. "We've probably killed more civilians than the enemy" someone said. No-one disagreed. I think it turned out to be a fact. Perhaps General Eisenhower knew more than us when he said, "Every foot at Caen lost to the enemy was worth ten miles anywhere else. Nothing must stand in the way." (Eisenhower 1944)

Just about fifty yards in front of us was a house, half destroyed, where I saw a tall, thin French lady emerge. She was dressed all in black with a black hat and carrying a large bag. She was having difficulty stepping over the rubble, so one of the soldiers went over to help her. At that, a News-reporter who was also sitting on the steps with us, took a photo of the soldier helping the French lady. Thirty years later someone lent me a war book simply called 'Caen' and on the front cover was that very photo. It brought back so many memories all those years later.

At this point in my story, things may be more difficult to record. Before Caen was taken it was reasonably easy to pick up on the important things and actions that the Brigade was involved in, as all three Regiments were always in close contact with each other. Although the story was intended to be about my own personal life and experiences, it is really not possible to exclude what was happening around me in the time of war.

It was obvious that the Division and the 185 Brigade would now be more engaged in pushing forward and keeping constant pressure on the Germans – this will restrict my story to what was happening immediately around me and my own Company.

After Caen, the Regiment was to re-group for our next action. The first thing I remember, after all these years, was that we moved to the east of Caen and very much more forward. My Company had to take position in a wood and to put our two-man dug-outs near the perimeter as defensive positions. It was a bit late in the day and the light was fading. We found it hard going to get anything like some depth to them owing to the roots of the trees, and on top of that it started to rain.

While we were engaged in digging, we could hear a German soldier constantly calling out, "Kamerad, Kamerad" and his voice was getting fainter. "Sounds like a German in need of help" said my friend. When the Platoon Sergeant appeared we asked him if we could go to his aid. "No!" he bellowed, "it may be a trick. Now listen to this – my orders to you now are not to take any prisoners." "Do you mean, Sergeant, that we shoot them even if they surrender?" "That's what I mean" he replied. Quite frankly this staggered us. This is not what the British Army does, I thought. Eventually the voice that kept calling "Kamerad" had faded away and stopped. We were sure that it was a wounded man. The tone of our Sergeant's voice seemed to be very angry and not his normal way.

After we eventually reached an acceptable depth in our dug-out it was quite dark, then we heard the two Cooks coming. "Get your Mess tins ready" one said. They appeared carrying a large container of hot stew and each of us received a big ladleful in our Mess tins. "What's up with the Sergeant?" we asked. "Oh, haven't you heard? The Canadians found a French prison in Caen and when they went in they found twenty four of their men and six of our Brigade tied up and with a bullet in the back of their heads." We were shocked, and that sort of thing really brought the truth home to us. I had heard many things about the cruelty of the Germans. I now understood the anger of our Sergeant. But the question was, would I be able to shoot a German who had given himself up?

The following day we were on the move again. It was evident that a big battle was going to take place involving the 185 Brigade along with a Tank Regiment. There were names like Manneville and Lirose, plus others I cannot now remember, but all in the battle area. It was planned that our Brigade and the 8th Infantry Brigade were to take part in this Operation. Very soon the time would come when the 3rd British Division and the 3rd Canadian Division would have to start really pushing the enemy back and for us to eventually fight them on their own soil.

It was planned that the K.S.L.I. would go into the attack mounted on the back of the Staffordshire Yeomanry tanks. No-one relished that as it could be quite dangerous. However we got into position and mounted the tanks and the Self-propelled Guns. The R.A.F. went into the attack first, then we set off. To ride on the backs of tanks was not the easiest thing to do, especially when there were about eight of us per tank.

We moved forward to the battle area and it was not long before the Germans realised the strength of our attack. Before we had gone far, we too came under fire. As we moved forward I noticed a large tree on the left of us about one hundred yards away and underneath there were about twenty or twenty five badly wounded German soldiers. I saw two of them with their arms outstretched as if calling for help. It looked as if they had been strafed by a British Fighter plane or perhaps a Typhoon rocket-firing plane. A sorrowful sight, but in war we just had to pass them by.

The enemy was now firing their Nebelwerfer Mortars at us as we approached. One landed quite close and injured one of the chaps on our tank – we had to hold him on as we dare not let him fall off because he could easily have been crushed by the armoured vehicles coming up behind us. We all dismounted as soon as the tanks stopped to go into the attack. It was a vicious battle with many wounded. I probably fired my rifle more times on that day than all the time I had been in France. The battle went on for quite some time until the enemy fell back. These battles were always costly in human life.

Our new Company Commander, Major Dane, was killed along with the Commander of Z Company, also Captain Kelly of W Company. It was a blow to the Battalion that we lost so many Officers, plus the Officers that were wounded in about three days of fighting. As a result of this battle, the loss of N.C.O.'s and other ranks was very high which took its toll on the Battalion, along with the rest of the Brigade, the Norfolk and the Warwickshire Regiments who also had it very rough.

Soon after, we moved to an area along the Railway – I cannot remember the name of the place but it was just after the battle of Manneville. Our Platoon was in a position after crossing the Railway line, where a section of our Platoon had to pass through a hedgerow where they came under fire. We then heard a call for the Stretcher-bearers and as they passed me with the wounded soldier, I immediately recognised him.

"Hi-ya Jonah" he called, "I've got a 'Blighty' – see you back in England – good old Blighty!" It was my Jewish friend, Abrahams. He had always hoped he would get a 'Blighty' wound. (A 'Blighty' wound is not serious, it's just enough to be sent back to England).

In 1983 I had the chance to go back and visit all the battle areas and I found something out which we were not aware of at the time.

Just off the coast of France at Arromanches, a Hospital ship was moored about half a mile out where certain of the wounded were treated. There were about two thousand people on board including the wounded, the Doctors, Nurses and the crew. I discovered that this ship was struck by either a Torpedo or a floating mine, and sadly it sank with a great loss of lives. I have often wondered if Abrahams ever did get back to Blighty or whether he suffered the same fate as those on the ship. I'll never know.

After the battles of the past, for a few weeks things seemed to be changing for the better, but we were never complacent about the enemy. I thought it was a rumour at first when we heard that X Company under Major Thornycroft had taken a Patrol many miles forward along a main road without meeting any opposition, giving rise to the thought that the enemy had fallen back a long way. Up until that point, owing to the fact we had advanced very quickly, some enemy units had been passed by and were actually behind us, but all these were soon dealt with.

With the reports that the Germans had fallen back, we advanced through most of Belgium unopposed. It was at this point when we stopped for a short break not too far from Brussels. We were in a position near some farms and I believed it was a question of re-organising again, when some of us had a pleasant surprise. Most of our Platoon was settling into a barn like building when the Platoon Sergeant came in and called out six names including mine. "Collect all your gear and hand it into the Q.M. Store vehicle" he said. He explained that we were to be given a break in turn starting with those who had been there the longest, i.e. the D-Day chaps. We did what he asked then all six of us were transported to a place in Brussels for a three night break.

We arrived at what looked like a disused hotel taken over by our Division for that purpose. We were greeted by a Corporal who was acting Janitor. "Right lads, I'll show you to your temporary quarters first then I'll show you the showers and give you all clean underwear and shirts etc. Get your showers and clean up – hand all the dirty clothes in then come down to the dining rooms and get a good meal." This was great and whilst in the dining room having a meal we were told that we were free to go out at night providing we were back by 10pm. The Corporal also explained to us that the Belgian people would come and speak to us and make a fuss of us but no way must we except offers of food from them as they had been short of food for a long time.

The chap in my room was a farm-hand back in England but he had a problem; when he laughed he had a high-pitched shrieking laugh and everyone could hear him – otherwise he was a really nice bloke. As lots of the places were beginning to open and some of the lights were now on in Brussels, we decided after dinner at about 7.30, we would go out together and try and find an English style Pub and chat to the Belgians. We also decided to ask the Cook if he had any spare grub he could give us to give any Belgian who befriended us. He gave us a tin of fruit as that was all he could spare, but I noticed he had some eggs in a basket. "Can I have a couple of those eggs, mate?" I asked. At first he said no, but then said, "O.K. but don't come for any more." Well, quite frankly, I took three and slid them into my Greatcoat pocket, and off we went.

It was getting a bit late as we walked along the main road in Brussels. "Keep a look out for a Pub or Bar" said my friend. Then up a side street I noticed what I thought was a Pub with coloured glass windows just like I had seen back home in Birmingham. "Are you sure it's a Pub?" asked my friend. "The only way to find out is to go in" I told him, so we walked in. It was very dimly lit and there were two chaps standing by the bar drinking. "There you are – what did I tell you!" I said. We sat down on a long leather covered seat under the window and were trying to sort out our bits of money when he nudged me and said, "This is not a Pub." "Of course it's a bloody Pub" I said. "Then take a look over there," and he pointed to a staircase in the corner. To my horror I saw two women in flimsy dressing gowns walking down the stairs! "Let's get out of here, quick!" whispered my friend – but too late – they came straight over and sat on our laps. "Buy me a drink, darling" one of the women said. In rather a confused voice I said, "No, I don't have enough money, thank you." Suddenly I realised something, and I pushed the woman off my lap so hard that she landed on the floor on her bottom. "What the bloody hell are you doing? You'll get us thrown out!" shouted the other chap. "Let's get out – let's get out!" I said, and I walked straight out followed by my confused friend. "What the bloody hell's the matter?" he asked frantically. "She sat on the bloody eggs and squashed the lot!" I explained angrily. Then my friend just stood against the wall shrieking with laughter as I stood on the edge of the pavement scraping the mess out of my pocket, whilst the women stood in the doorway cursing us in Flemish! Well, that was the first and last experience I had had in a 'house of ill repute.' It was the topic of conversation for the next three days. We were then picked up and taken back to the Regiment.

It was a great relief and pleasure to travel by Army transport through some of the towns with thousands of happy Belgians cheering us through. I am not sure how I came to be in the back of the Food Lorry with the Cooks etc., but as we were going through at a rather slow speed, I well remember three young girls keeping up with us. One of the Cooks sorted out a half empty four-pint tin of jam. He leaned over the tail-board and handed it to the girls. They continued to keep up with us but at the same time all three kept dipping their fingers into the jam and putting it in their mouths! It was indeed a happy moment for them and us.

After all the celebrations we eventually stopped near the Escant Canal where things changed dramatically. First the whole Battalion re-equipped as it was obvious that things were going to get hard again. We did a certain amount of re-training bringing back the reality that the fight was not over yet. In late September two Companies crossed the Canal in Assault Boats to form a foothold on the other side but they came under very heavy fire, proving the enemy were making a stand. Sadly there were a number of casualties. Two Officers were killed and about twenty other ranks were killed or wounded. Our Company was then sent over to try and form the Bridgehead, but the enemy was still in strength and a number of casualties resulted. It was a sad time for the Battalion again with the amount of losses we incurred.

The following morning reports came through via civilians, that the Germans had gone. The Battalion again re-grouped and moved to a place in Holland where the 11th Armoured Division had crossed the Canal. We then met up with the Hereford Regiment who were holding the Bridgehead, so three of our Companies were sent across the Canal leaving one Company back at the crossing point. The weather was now terrible. It was pouring with rain and everywhere was waterlogged.

There were dead Germans all over the place – in ditches, in the woods, in fact everywhere just rotting – as a result of their counter attack on the Armoured Brigade.

At the end of September the U.S. Army came up to take over the area, which allowed us to go back for two nights giving the Battalion a short break.

A reconnaissance party was sent forward to check the area. Soon after the Battalion followed and moved forward. We were now about a mile and a half from the German border and not far from the River Maas. This whole area was being held by the U.S. Airborne Division who had held it since the British had landed at Arnhem. They seemed very relieved and glad that we were taking over. I just felt I wanted to get into a dug-out and go to sleep! It had been a very trying couple of weeks with the bad weather making it all the worse. However it seemed to be getting warmer and more acceptable in early October. We were still being shelled and as a result there were more casualties.

Once again a reconnaissance party was sent out as it appeared that there were some small Dutch towns the Division would have to capture. One was Overloon, another was Venray, and some others whose names I forget. These proved to be amongst some of the hardest battles with bad weather again. The conditions of the battle at Overloon were extreme– everywhere was deep mud which made movement difficult and everyone was wet and muddy. The enemy did not seem to relent with their defence of it which created more casualties, some of whom had to be kept in the cellars of some larger houses.

I have said in the earlier part of my story that I always wanted to be on Transport as I had passed my driving test at Shrewsbury and it was entered into my Pay book. It had just stopped raining when a Sergeant called out, "Jones, have you a Drivers Pass?" "Yes Sergeant, it's in my Pay book." "O.K. then – one of the drivers has been wounded and I want you to take some Officers to a meeting" he ordered. I tried to explain I had not driven for eighteen months, but he said, "Don't argue, Lad, get going!" He pointed to a 15 cwt. Ford truck, as four Officers came over. They had arranged to meet other Officers about one mile back, for a conference on the situation. I jumped into the driver's seat feeling a bit out of place. I almost said to myself, 'well, that's what I wanted – now stop worrying.' I soon got the hang of it again and off I went down the main street. The shelling had been quite bad and I had only gone a hundred yards when the shelling started again and Mortar shells were dropping in the street in front of us. One Officer wanted me to stop to take shelter, but the Senior Officer said, "Carry on as fast as you can." The problem was there were holes and rubble in the road. However, we reached a cross-road and one Officer pointed out to me the place they wanted. It was a small church which seemed to be a safe place. I had to wait nearly two hours before I took them back again. I then reported to the Sergeant who said, "Leave the truck behind that building and get back into position." That was the nearest I got to driving transport for some time.

The shelling from the Germans seemed to be getting less the day after, but our own bombardment was more intense. It was felt that the Germans were beginning to weaken, but our Gunners never seemed to let up with our Bofors guns. The battles in the Dutch areas were some of the worst and it tried every man. Venray was also a very intense battle. Whilst Y Company moved round to a place called Oostrum, something happened there which also made me remember it well.

The general conditions over the past few weeks reminded me of my father's experiences in the Battle of the Somme and how he coped in all those long periods of fighting which were so much more severe.

After a couple of days at Oostrum, in the late afternoon about six of us with an N.C.O. were asked to go further into the town near to a factory from where it was suspected we were being observed. Almost immediately we were fired upon so it was decided to go a slightly different route through a couple of buildings that were badly damaged. Two of the men climbed over the crumbling wall then I was given a leg-up onto it, when the wall collapsed. I was stuck with a badly damaged ankle – the same one I had damaged in Scotland. After the others did their recce. they helped me back to our original position and I was immediately put into a jeep and driven off. It was quite dark by then and after a couple of miles we came to a make-shift Hospital which was a small school that had been commandeered by the Army for minor injuries. The driver helped me in and dumped me on a long bench in the hallway and reported to a Medical Orderly. My overcoat was damp and covered with mud, also my trousers and boots; plus I had not had a wash or clean up for weeks – I looked a proper sight in this place! I lay full length on the bench to rest myself and fell fast asleep.

Soon afterwards, I was woken up by the Orderly. "Here you are, Mate – get this down ya" He had brought me a nice mug of hot tea. "Drink that and I'll come and see to you." After a short while he helped me up and took me into a room where there were four Army bunks two of which were occupied. He helped me onto a bunk and took off my Greatcoat and proceeded to remove my boots. Then came a voice from the opposite bunk. "Hi-ya Jonah, got yourself a 'Blighty'?" Well, I was amazed – it was one of the lads from the Copthorne Camp in Shrewsbury who'd joined at the same time as me. "No" I shouted, "I fell off a wall while on a recce!" "You jammy bastard" was his reply.

The Orderly took my boots off and my socks then my trousers. I felt awful as my socks and feet were filthy. "Sorry" I said, "I've not had a bath for weeks." "Don't worry Mate, everyone's the same; it can't be helped." He then washed my feet and legs with warm water. "I'll get the Medic now to have a look at you; your ankle is quite swollen." At that he put my Greatcoat, trousers and boots on the floor next to the bed and went off. Shortly afterwards an Officer Medic came in and examined my ankle. "Yes, you've damaged the ball of the joint but we'll soon fix you up." He called the N.C.O. Medic to strap my ankle up and cover it with plaster. "You'll have to keep that plaster on for a few days" he remarked. When he disappeared, I called over to the chap I knew. "I think these chaps deserve a medal for the dirty jobs they have to do!" "Well, that bloke who fixed you up had to get a piece of shrapnel out of my arse! How would you like to do that?" was the reply. Shortly after, as it was about 10pm they brought us a cup of hot cocoa and once again I fell fast asleep. I woke up in the morning with the smell of cooking. I saw the Orderly standing there with a metal plate and on it was a lump of bread and a couple of fried fish cakes and a mug of tea. "Blimey, what time is it?" I asked. "Ten o'clock. Didn't you hear the shelling last night? One dropped about a hundred yards away!" he said.

Another Orderly was sweeping the floor; it had been covered in mud which had since dried up and there were bits of bandage and all sorts on the floor. In Civvy Street it would have been condemned for the mess, but these chaps were doing a marvellous job under the circumstances. I noticed that my Greatcoat, boots and trousers had gone. "Where are my clothes, Mate?" I asked. "Oh don't worry about them; we have a few Civvy volunteers who come in for a few hours and they're probably giving them a brush down for you."

During the time I was there I had lots of time to think as my mind was a lot clearer. I thought of what the chap over in the opposite bed had said to me when I told him what was wrong with me. "You jammy bastard!" he had said to me. Well I could not argue with that when I thought back to all the things that had happened and the close shaves I had experienced, and the terrible things we had all had to witness which was all part of the war.

When Infantry soldiers are asked what part of the Army they are in, usually they reply "P.B.I.'s" which is short for 'poor bloody Infantry' and is supposed to be the measure of the unpleasant job they have to do. I have thought of this many times and come to realise that other soldiers have a worse job to do and those are the ones who have to go round and clean up the terrible mess after the battles, such as the men who have to sort out the bodies, some of which have been lying for weeks and may be dismembered. Some bodies have to be removed from burned out tanks and armoured vehicles. I, as many of us, had to witness all these situations and I know I could not do that job. To me, their job was far worse than mine.

CHAPTER TWELVE

After a few days I was able, and allowed, to walk about. The pain and swelling had subsided. My clothes and boots had been returned and I found them in a reasonably clean state when I awoke the following morning, but I never knew who had cleaned them. The chap I knew and I went out a couple of times and walked around the village. The Dutch were very kind to us and showed their thanks and appreciation. Some of them offered to take us into their houses and give us soup. However, we definitely had to refuse as they had been starving themselves for a long time under the German occupation – but we thanked them nonetheless.

After six days, the Medic came and removed the plaster and strapping, gave me a good check-over and said, "Tomorrow I will arrange to get you picked up." The next day, just after mid-day, one of the drivers from the Battalion showed up. "You O.K. now Mate?" he asked. "Yes thanks – let's go" I said. "We've a few miles to go" he told me "the Battalion is at Rijkevoort. The weather has been terrible – the whole place is deep in filthy mud." It was a difficult drive, slipping and sliding down muddy roads and lanes, some partly blocked with Army vehicles. I did not like the look of it at all.

"Right, Mate, that's your lot over there" the driver said. He dropped me outside a make-shift Company Head Quarters which looked like an old farm building that had been forgotten about for years. "Thanks Mate" I said as he drove off. A couple of N.C.O.'s stood outside – "Well, well" they said, "look who's here." They gave me a mug of tea and told me all that had happened whilst I was away. "We shall be moving on when the lads have been rested" they told me, and took me to the edge of a wood as it was just starting to get dark. There was a row of two-man slit-trenches all with covers on made out of old doors etc. and covered with soil. "That's your pitch" said one of the N.C.O.'s pointing to a slit-trench. I climbed in and was greeted by a chap brewing a mug of tea. "Hiya Mate, fancy a cuppa?" Well, how could I refuse?

I knew this chap by sight but had never had the chance to talk to him. "I'm Harry" he said. "I'm Ron" I told him and we shook hands. He was one of the Regulars from Lockerbie. "It's nice and warm in here" I said. "Yes, but there's snow on the way" he replied. "Fancy going out later? I know where there is a cinema close by." He explained that we were free to do as we pleased as we were resting, and also said that an E.N.S.A. show was near by too, although it was nearly wrecked by shell fire a couple of night before. Luckily no-one was hurt.

"The first thing is to go and get some grub – there's an old barn a couple of hundred yards away which is our temporary Cook-house and it's time to go" said Harry. When we got there quite a number of chaps were sitting on straw bales eating their supper. I held out my two Mess tins – a large sausage, a boiled egg and a lump of bread went in one tin and the usual helping of hot char in the other. A couple of lads in my Platoon acknowledged me but I think they were too interested in their grub to chat. I said to Harry that it would be something of a novelty to say we went to a cinema in between battle periods, so when we finished our meal he took me to what looked like the centre of a small village nearby and sure enough there was a small cinema. I cannot remember what we paid, or even whether we paid, but it was a nice little cinema inside, and although a few soldiers were already in there, we still were looked at by the Dutch civilians as we sat down – but more so when I lit a cigarette! "You can't smoke in here" said my friend, "it's not allowed." Almost as soon as he had said that, a Dutch attendant came and told me that I couldn't smoke. I had no objection if that was the rule, and I remembered the saying, 'when in Rome do as the Romans do.' I thought it a pity that the rule didn't seem to apply in England. However I enjoyed the hour in the cinema – Dutch films with English sub-titles.

The walk back to our dug-out was a bit of an ordeal though with the damp fog and being bad underfoot.

The following night seven of us plus an N.C.O. were detailed for a patrol. It seemed a regular thing in this area and we could still hear the occasional gun fire not too far away – and the snow had started to fall.

I think it was about the 18th of December when the whole Brigade had to take positions along the River Maas; the Norfolks in one area, the 2nd K.S.L.I. in another and the Warwickshire Regiment further downstream. We in Y Company were probably a little more fortunate in our position. The place was called Lottrum.

The first thing I noticed was a very large, what I would describe as Victorian, house very much English in style. As I had not been detailed for any immediate duty I was tempted to look the house over. Unfortunately I had a bit of a problem as I was suffering from a skin rash in my groin, owing to the continuous wet and cold weather and the fact that I had been unable to get a proper bath and a change of underwear since I came out of the temporary Hospital. I was in need of a good shower and change of under clothes.

Upstairs in this old house was a four-poster bed already laid out by the previous occupiers, and there was a very large chest of drawers full of clean linen – so under the circumstances I had a good look to see if there was any men's underwear but the only thing I could find was a drawer full of women's knee-length white knickers all neatly pressed and folded. I knew it would be a couple of weeks before some Army supplies would arrive, so I took hold of a pair. Also upstairs was a very large, cold bathroom. Well I could not wait any longer so I stripped off, half filled the bath with cold water and stood in it. With the aid of some small scraps of soap I found plus my shaving soap, I had a good, but very cold, wash down. After drying myself I very reluctantly put on the knickers which had to be tied up with fine silk tape. Once fully dressed I felt great – and clean! It was a few days before I told the lads what I had done and I cannot say here what remarks were made!! It was a couple of weeks before we had some proper clean underwear delivered and were told to hand in our dirty clothes. I will always remember the Quarter Master's face when I handed him the women's knee-length knickers for cleaning!!

We all had to do patrol duties and look-out duties while we were there, which took us well past Christmas and we got to know the terrain very well. There was a path about 250 yards long from the house leading to the river. We had dug trenches for look-out purposes at various distances from the river. All around the property were piglets running around wild and chickens which were laying eggs in the small buildings outside, so we had an abundance of food if we needed it, especially as our Platoon Sergeant was a butcher by trade.

On Christmas Day, two of us were detailed to do look-out duty in a two-man dug-out near the river. Things had been pretty quiet on our Section with little or no contact with the enemy so we were quite happy about that, but the snow and general conditions made it quite uncomfortable at times. Sitting there on Christmas Day, miles from home in a cold dug-out was though we had been forgotten. Then round about lunchtime two of the lads came walking towards us each carrying a large oval plate covered with a towel. When they handed them to us we had a very pleasant surprise. On the plates was a pile of pork meat, two or three roasted chicken legs, four fried eggs each and some vegetables which must have been out of a tin. There was also a little note saying, 'Merry Christmas from the Sergeant.' That was a real uplift for Christmas Day. That was something else I have always remembered about that place on the Maas.

The previous night we had heard someone singing Carols from over the river. We did not know whether it was the Germans or the Dutch. What we could not understand was why the enemy were continuing to fight as it was obvious to us all that they had no chance – whatever they threw at us, we would give them back double. They must have suffered an appalling loss of life.

One night after Christmas I was on patrol in a different part of the river bank. No matter how careful we were we could not notice everything. We had gone about 100 yards along the edge of the river when one of us set off a trip flare. It shot into the air about 200 feet and burst into bright daylight. All six of us stood there motionless as we had been trained. Fortunately there were a lot of shrubs in the area which I believe had camouflaged us and not a shot was fired, but we never moved until the flare hit the ground and fizzled out. Once again I considered we had been very lucky not to be spotted.

During these times although conditions could be most uncomfortable on occasions, we could get a laugh out of circumstances which relieved the tension. Unlike the men in the First World War who were bogged down for months at a time, in our war we moved around more often which eased the strain and even in action certain things could happen which would put a smile on a face.

In this area our Platoon was positioned for a temporary defence or look-out. We were in two-man dug-outs spaced about 25 feet apart. I had a Corporal with me. There was snow all around us so we were wearing balaclavas and mittens to keep warm. It was about two o'clock in the morning – a clear sky and frosty. The Corporal kept complaining he needed a toilet and could not wait. "Sod this" he said and made for a bush about 20 feet in front of us. Almost as soon as he had hidden himself, the two men in the dug-out on my left had spotted a possible enemy patrol about 250 yards away. So I threw some snowballs at the bushes to alert the Corporal, much to his anger and he shouted swear words at me not realising I was trying to attract his attention. This started a chain of events as the chaps in the trench on my right who were nearer to the bushes quickly told him of the danger and suddenly he came scampering back with his trousers half down, and dived back into the dug-out. Then the chaps in the other trench called to say the possible enemy patrol had disappeared. We all had a good snigger – except the Corporal who had had his pride hurt, but with a grin on his face he gave us a bit of a rollicking in the morning – he had seen the funny side of it!

Things there remained quiet on our Section, but not so with others. We heard an explosion one night, coming from Z Company area. We found out that their Company Commander and an N.C.O. had been killed and many others wounded. They had been investigating something that had been Booby-trapped.

At the end of December we were on the move again. We moved to an area held by the Monmouthshire Regiment at a place called Roermond. We took over a small wood which ran alongside the Wilhems Canal. We received lots of attention from the enemy guns but we returned their fire two-fold. Along this stretch of the Canal were some small buildings and on our Company's section was a cottage which we used as a look-out – it was probably a Lock-Keepers cottage, and we took turns there to be on duty. I think it was the second day when I with two others used it.

The main window had all of the glass removed; it left a wall about thirty inches high underneath and the wall either side of the open window were about four feet wide, so we could lie down below the window with safety and stand up either side. This opening looked in the direction of the Canal and we could also see the roofs of some buildings partly hidden by trees. In the distance a church steeple could be seen quite clearly. Between us we had two rifles and a Bren gun with plenty of ammunition. After a while of observation, the other rifleman said, "I have been watching the lower half of that steeple – one minute I look and I think there is a tile missing, next time I look it isn't." We were all concerned about that in case someone was observing us from there. All three of us concentrated on this spot and after a while we decided a tile was being removed occasionally, so we decided to give it a burst with the Bren gun to see what happened. About ten good shots were fired hitting the steeple at the lower section. We then lay on the floor below the window level and after a few minutes a burst of machine-gun fire came through the window, smashing a large wardrobe standing against the back wall behind us. The Bren gunner put a new magazine of ammunition in his gun and fired the complete magazine-full at the steeple, then another magazine-full at the tops of the other buildings we could just see. No more bullets came our way again that day.

We left this area towards the end of January. The time there had been very active and Second-Lieutenant Francis won the Military Cross for defending the house he was in. Although he was wounded he killed many of the enemy and had driven off the attack.

The conditions now were very bad because of the dampness, the snow and the foggy weather which was making everything unpleasant underfoot. There is one thing I can say here though – all the time I was in the Army and with all the conditions we had to put up with, I never once had blisters or problems with my feet. However there were many of the lads who did suffer with their feet!

We were given a bit of relaxation from the fighting as we were going to train for the crossing of the River Maas, but for some reason which I do not know, that was cancelled. Instead we were to train with the Buffalo Regiment – a Regiment of Amphibious vehicles – to cross the River Rhine. This was something that had to be done with great care as the Rhine is a very wide river and very strong as at that time of the year was full and running fast.

With all this work, I had forgotten about my 20th birthday on the 10th of February. I only realised it when someone else remarked,

"Fancy having to do this on your 22nd birthday!" "What day is it then?" I asked him. "It's the bloody 19th of February" he replied. It's the thing that happens to us all in the Forces especially during war times. The good thing is, I am still around to think about it!!

With all the briefing going on, it was obvious to us that we were going into battle again. We, the 185 Brigade, had to reach the Rhine starting at Goch and Pfalzdorf and eventually Kervenheim. This last place is a name I have always remembered. We were told it was held by a Regiment of German Paratroopers so the thought of it being easy was out of our minds although most of the men still could not understand why the Germans continued fighting.

At the end of February it all started. We had to advance through thick woodland and soon came under fire. It became very difficult to clear a way through these woods, not just because of the enemy but the difficult conditions as it all seemed like bog land and we eventually reached a point where it was getting too dark to continue. The only thing to do was stop and set up a defensive position. It gave us a chance to get a bite to eat and something to drink.

It was early morning on the 1st of March. Our Company moved forward to the inside edge of the wood and at about 7am as we waited for the word to go, we could see a row of farm buildings on our right. Immediately ahead was a grass field covered in very tall grass and after that some buildings on the outskirts of the town. It looked as though we would have to attack through open ground. I'm not exactly sure what time it was when all of the Platoon I was with were ordered to line up and fan out as we moved into the open. The buildings on our right curved across to our front at about 45 degrees so when we were ordered to advance we had to slightly wheel to our right. "O.K." said the Platoon Sergeant, "are you all ready? Let's go!" As we moved out, each man was about eight feet apart and the enemy started to fire almost immediately, the rifle and light machine-gun fire cutting through the tall grass past our legs and feet. As we could not at that time see where this fire was coming from, the best policy was to travel forward as fast as we could whilst firing from the hip. In this way, at least plenty of fire from us would keep their heads down.

We had gone about a hundred yards when a most unusual thing happened. There was a large house to our right and the next house forward was about a hundred yards in front of that one. All of a sudden about twelve or fifteen German soldiers ran across open ground to the house in front, which meant they had to sprint this distance with their weapons. We could only think that they had not noticed our Platoon. We all quickly took aim and fired and I do not think any of them made it to that house – it was almost as though they committed suicide – they had made a terrible mistake and paid the price.

As the Platoon got to within about fifteen feet of the row of houses, an enemy shell dropped quite near and the chap on my left was struck on the top of his thigh with a piece of shrapnel, though he was not seriously hurt. "Get into that farmhouse" I said to him, "we'll get the Medics to you later." The others started to go through the gaps between the houses, but I followed the wounded man into the building. In the hallway was a large bench seat which I made him lie on. "You haven't got a serious wound" I told him, "so stay here and we'll send a Medic to you." I was about to go out of the back door when he said quietly, "I can hear voices in here, Ron." But I could not hear clearly after the noise outside. There was a door in the hallway which I noticed was slightly open, so I looked in. There were some steps leading to a cellar and I saw a glow from a paraffin lamp. I shouted out, "English soldier!" and to my amazement a German Medical Officer came to the bottom of the stairs with his hands up and holding a card with a red cross on it. I pointed my rifle at him and he pleaded with me not to shoot him as he had a wounded soldier in the cellar. I crept down with a hand-grenade in one hand and sure enough there was a badly wounded German soldier on a stretcher and also five German Paratroopers standing against the wall with their hand up. The one said how glad he was to be taken prisoner by an English soldier and not a Russian one. I was furious with myself as I had made a bad mistake just going into a building like that. However it was obvious they had had enough and they pointed to all their weapons on the floor with all the ammunition taken out.

The Medical Officer begged me to allow them to carry their wounded comrade upstairs to get him into the light to attend to him. I ordered him to do it quickly as I had to leave to join my Company outside. They did this straight away and laid him, still on the stretcher, in the hallway near the door. I then ordered the others to sit up against the wall with their hands on their heads which they did, and seemed glad it was all over. I spoke to my friend and told him there was nothing to worry about and I would get help straight away. I started to walk to the back door when suddenly a shell hit the wall above the front door and half the front wall over the door collapsed. Then a British tank appeared aiming its cannon down the hall. I was looking down its bloody barrel!! I was uncontrollably furious when I saw the tank Commander, with a big red bushy moustache, looking like a bloody 'Biggles' sitting out of the top of the tank. I was so angry to think I could have been killed by my own side. "You stupid idiot!" I called to him, and asked him if that was his job to go round shooting up a building which had already been captured by the Infantry. I was actually shaking with temper and the Germans were looking on, listening to the argument. This guy threatened to have me charged for my insolence and I replied, "If that's all you have to do, you can look after this lot, Mate." I then quickly hopped out of the back door and caught up with the rest of the Platoon who had about another twenty prisoners and were about to attack another row of buildings further in the town.

Two more of our Platoon were wounded in the attack and there were many casualties during the day on both sides, but eventually as hard as the Germans fought they had no chance of stopping our Brigade and other supporting troops. Later in the evening I heard that in Z Company a Private Joseph Stokes had won the Victoria Cross for his actions. I wondered what had possessed this man to do what he did. He was wounded a number of times, but still attacked the enemy and continued to do so and died in this action on the field.

I will never forget this battle. The enemy were fighting on their own soil and it was well understood why they fought so hard. Like many other battles many a brave man had died there that day, both British and German.

Kervenheim was still not completely captured until a Canadian Brigade came through. We managed to get a bit of rest during this time, but early next morning the Armoured Troop Carriers arrived to take us into battle again at a place called Kapellen. The path was almost blocked with tanks, Armoured Vehicles and S.P. Guns ready for this final push to the Rhine. We were being shelled all the way and learned that Captain Wilson had been killed and two young Lieutenants had been wounded.

Our Company had to dismount to attack a ridge near to the town. A section of this was wooded so as before, we went in firing from the hip so we could move fast and keep the Germans' heads down. Surprisingly we did not get much coming back at us until we were on the edge of the wood. Suddenly something hit me on my right side almost spinning me around – I didn't know what it was until later when I had chance to look. I couldn't see any blood so I wasn't too concerned, but discovered later that a bullet had gone through my right pouch striking my webbing belt on the way through, leaving a groove about two inches long in the belt! If it had hit me square on it would have gone right into me – it was a glancing blow. But many men had such close shaves like that and got away with it!

With the aid of a few of our shells we were able to move on and get closer to the Rhine. There was a lot of flat land along the banks of the Rhine and the river was running fast and nearly up to the top of the banks. We stayed well back for a time where there was some cover. After we had settled down, some of us were detailed to dig trenches forward of the Company position and I was told to dig mine by a line of fencing.

Shortly after, the Platoon Sergeant brought a young new Reserve to me and asked me to show him what to do. This young chap had not been in action before so I had to explain a few things to him. He spoke perfect English and seemed very well educated. When we had finished digging the trench we had a chance to talk. "What's your name?" I asked. "Peter Potter" he replied. I thought it was a bit unusual, a name like that, and I enquired what he did in Civvy Street. "I was in college until I was called up – I'm studying to be a script-writer, the same as my father who does work for the B.B.C." he said. Now I knew why he was well-spoken, and I wondered what he thought of my 'Brummie' accent! He was very polite and offered me a cigarette which I accepted but told him, "Don't light up after dark." He then questioned me about the situation and why we had dug the trench. "We are going to cross the Rhine in the morning, but before that there will be an Artillery Barrage. This trench is just for our protection if any shells drop short or if the enemy send some over." After that we talked a great deal – he seemed a very nice chap and wanted to know everything. He did not seem a bit nervous – or did not show it. Later on we had some hot tea brought to us. I felt very sleepy but under the circumstances I could not allow myself to sleep, so I told Peter to have a nap if he could. "No, I don't think I could!" he told me.

The Artillery Guns had been set up behind us and like us all, were waiting for orders. I was not sure of the time – very few Infantry Privates carried watches – but each Artillery crew fired one round each to line up their guns. After about another fifteen minutes they repeated this. I explained to Peter that they did this to make sure they were on target before the actual Barrage started. Somehow, the time did not seem important to us – it was to the planners of the battles that time was important. Some time in the early hours the real Barrage began. It's a noise that's difficult to explain; perhaps a near earthquake might be the best way to describe it. It went on for a very long time and one wonders about those who are receiving it. The devastation caused by such Barrages is just as indescribable.

Eventually the Barrage just stopped and all was quiet except for the noise of moving transport. The Amphibious Craft were lining up for us to mount – about twenty eight or thirty men to each Craft, which all moved together when the order was given to go. The last obstacle, we all thought. It was early morning and starting to get light. The Craft plunged onto the river which was high and very wide and running fast. It was impossible to keep the Craft on a straight course with the pull of the river. When we hit the bank on the far side we were probably about 150 yards further down-stream. When our Craft contacted the bank, it lurched to one side and was wedged over at a steep angle which was quite worrying – so we did not need to be told to get out quickly; our training again told us to act speedily.

The ground was flat so we could move fast and the Platoon fanned out and started to advance towards the town. There was a small road directly ahead with damaged houses on both sides. The first people we saw were an elderly woman screaming her head off and a young girl trying to calm her and drag her into a house. I'm not sure whether she was suffering from the shelling or was thinking we would shoot her – there was no chance of that. We moved very quickly down the street and into the town, meeting little or no opposition.

The most dangerous part of that day was the crossing of the river. With the condition of it and the speed, no-one could have survived with all their equipment on had they fallen into the water. However that did not happen and I don't think anyone thought about it until they were over. In fact to be truthful, as no shots were fired to my knowledge, it seemed like a practice run apart from the earlier Barrage.

At this point I have to say it is difficult for me to remember exactly all that was happening and the names of the small towns and villages, as we were moving about so quickly from one place to another, in fact it seemed as if half the British Army was in the area. There were tanks, Bren gun carriers, Troop transporters and S.P. Guns everywhere.

It did not seem long before the Brigade was on its way back across the Rhine. This I do remember as our Company came back over by rail on a bridge that looked as if it had been put over by the Royal Engineers, but I could not be certain about that. We all felt good that we were now back in Holland amongst friendly people who were always ready to speak of their appreciation for us having driven the enemy from their country. We were glad to have a short rest and get cleaned up with showers and fresh clothes and good meals.

All this did not last long though before we were in action again in Germany. There was a lot of activity everywhere. Now, as I write this book late on in life, trying to recall what was done and the names of places, especially as we were on the move so often, I can only write about the main things I can remember as honestly as I can.

Dortmund was now the battle plan, but the Dortmund Canal and the river were probably the two main obstacles. I do well remember the Company moving up to the Canal through a wooded area. When we came through to the edge of the wood, there was the Canal, and immediately on our right were a group of Engineers putting the finishing touches to a steel bridge across the Canal. It looked wide enough and strong enough to get medium vehicles over. As our Platoon was the closest to it, four of us including me, were asked – or should I say detailed – to do a quick Recce over the Canal and into the wood on the other side. As it appeared to be rather quiet at that time of the morning, I was not too worried – but I thought I had learned before this to keep out of the way before I was detailed for Recce's! However, the four of us trotted over the bridge to get the job done quickly. We fanned out and went separate ways. I went to the extreme left and at about 150 yards in, I noticed what I thought was a hideaway – it was a pile of branches up against a tree and covered all over with twigs and leaves for camouflage. The first thing that came to my mind was it was booby-trapped, so I gently lifted a lot of the twigs off with the aid of my rifle and bayonet, looking all the time for wire or string. When I had lifted enough off, I looked inside and there was a shiny black car the like of which I had never seen before, but I know now as a V.W. Beetle! I was fascinated by this and I had to have a closer look. Someone must have put it there for safety – it was brand new, but it was the shape that was so interesting. I left it covered over and got on with the Recce.

As I walked further into the wood, I spotted a small group of people coming towards me. There was a tall, smartly dressed man, a middle-aged woman pushing a pram, a little girl about ten years old and, what really interested me, a very short, stocky man in a greenish uniform. I instructed them to get in front of me and took them back over the bridge, but not knowing who the man in the uniform was, I told him to put his hands up. At this the tall German man said, "Kamerad – Kamerad" but I had come this far and I was not going to take any chances. I asked him again but he did not understand until I poked him with my bayonet. I took them back and handed them over to an Officer who interrogated them. After a few minutes, the Officer told me that the man in uniform was an escaped Russian prisoner. "Oh, I know now why he scowled at me when I poked him in the ribs!" I said. "Is there anything else to report?" he asked. I told him about the lovely car I'd found, and he said, "It sounds like something I could use as a runabout vehicle – could you find it again?" "No problem" I told him. "Good, I will have a look at it when we all go over" he said.

It was rather puzzling at this stage as our Regiment never did cross at this point. It appeared that another Regiment had crossed the Canal and also the river. It also seemed that we were looking for the enemy and many Patrols were organised to search them out. Many thousands of Germans had given themselves up or had been captured by that time. Even though this was the situation we were still receiving the occasional shells dropping near us and very often hitting their target, which told us that there were many Germans still prepared to stand and defend their country.

Once again our Company seemed to be separated from the main Battalion and were with Headquarters at Lemfoerde. It was fairly quiet at this small town and reasonable restful, but there were many pockets of resistance for the rest of the Companies to deal with whilst we were taking care of a place called Sudweyhe.

It was coming up to late April – even in the midst of warfare something sometimes happens to be looked upon as funny or unusual. Whilst we were in this small area we were still detailed for Recce work. On a local Patrol, six of us came across a small work-shop for repairing motor-bikes etc. In there was a small two-stroke motor-bike in lovely condition so we decided to bring it back as a little runabout or to have a bit of fun with, as things were quiet. We mixed some two-stroke fuel, filled the tank and started the engine up which ran perfectly. The following day it was left lying against the wall of our temporary Cookhouse. The Sergeant, who I have mentioned before was a butcher by trade, always seemed to organise the grub while we were detached from the Battalion. He called me over to talk to me and said, "Hey, Jones, do you think you could knock up a trailer for that little motor-bike?" "What ever for?" I asked. "We are moving to another little village tomorrow and we thought we could take a few of these chickens that are running about wild." I could hardly believe this, but I knew he was not a man to joke about things. "Right, O.K. I'll see what I can do" I said, still feeling a bit surprised.

After searching around, we found a small two-handled barrow. We fixed a bar with a rail across the end of the handles then wrapped some wire around that and attached it to the back of the saddle – it worked perfectly! The following morning I found some wire mesh to put on the top of the trailer to keep the chickens from jumping out. A few of the lads were running about trying to catch the chickens and eventually we had eight altogether in the barrow and soon all of them had their heads sticking out of the wire mesh.

The Convoy had started to assemble and get ready to move. There were Troop Transporters, Bren gun Carriers, Anti-tank Guns, a couple of Officers' Jeeps, the Medics' vehicle and at the back was a Despatch Rider. I was to bring up the rear with the bike and trailer full of chickens. 'I'm going to look a right idiot riding at the back of the Convoy with this lot' I thought. I pulled up behind the last vehicle, thinking 'thank God I've only a few miles to go.' The Despatch Rider pulled up beside me and gave me a funny look. "God" he said, "you've got a bloody nerve!" "Orders are orders, mate!" I replied, and the Convoy moved forward. The road was fairly narrow and a couple of hundred yards ahead we had to do a left hand turn at a tee-junction. At the junction was a Military Police soldier making sure we all went the right way. By him was a British News reporter with his cameras. I have often wondered if he took a picture of a soldier on a red motor-bike towing a trailer full of confused chickens!!

We had only travelled a few miles when we came to the next village where we were to make camp. I had to drop my cargo of chickens where the Cookhouse was intended to be and that was the last I saw of them. This place was more wooded than the one we had just left. We could hear gun-fire some distance away, so the first thing to do, no matter how quiet it seemed, was to sort our defensive positions and dig trenches again. Later in the day Recce Patrols were being organised.

The following afternoon I was detailed for a Patrol and there was to be a whole Section of us as we were going to look for any enemy resistance. The Patrol consisted of a Second Lieutenant who I'd not seen before in our Platoon, an N.C.O. and eleven men. We were going to patrol along the open road, so one man would be positioned about fifty to one hundred yards ahead, and one man the same distance at the rear – that was to be my position, the tail man. The road was not a very wide one and it went up a slight incline bearing to the left in a big loop. The right hand side was partially wooded with occasional small houses, and on the left, where we had to walk because we had a better view, there was a hedgerow and the land the other side swept down to a shallow valley. The Officer estimated it was probably about a mile and a half in total. It was a nice spring evening – one of the best days we had had for some time, so we were in good spirit and the scenery was good too.

I was about fifty yards behind as required and had to look in all directions and sometimes stop for a few seconds to listen. It was quiet and peaceful except for distant gun and rifle fire. As we started round the bend at the top, everything looked nicer with the ground on the left sloping away to the valley. There were one or two houses on the right of the road but were all found to be empty after a search by the main patrol. When we reached the top of the road the light was beginning to fade as the evening came on. I then had to stop as nature called and I had to relieve myself. I was standing by the hedge when I was sure I could hear footsteps following up behind us, but some distance away. I went on a further one hundred yards then stopped to listen again. It could have been one of our own Patrols but I didn't think they would send another group on the same route, so I hurried up to the last man of the main Patrol and asked him to pass the message up to the Lieutenant. He waited until the Patrol was level with two houses on the far side, set back into the wood, and we all went through the hedge and lay down in the field whilst observing the road.

After a while the footsteps became clearer and it was obvious they were all in step. As I was on the end of the Patrol I would be the first to see who they were. The Officer meantime had moved to the middle of our group. Then I spotted six German soldiers with weapons, who slowly made their way across the road and went through the side door of one of the houses opposite. The Officer told all of us to have our rifles pointing at the windows and doors but not to fire unless he ordered it. He then put single shot of his own through one of the windows and shouted out to tell them to surrender – but nothing happened, though we could hear them talking. He gave them a couple of minutes then ordered us to put one shot each through the windows. After a few seconds, the Officer said, "They're thinking about it; now keep me covered." He calmly walked over the road, kicked the door hard and told them to surrender. By that time we had surrounded the place. The door opened and they came out with their hands up – only one of them had been wounded. Six of us stood and held the Germans while the rest went into the building. "Gather all the weapons and the ammunition including those stick-grenades and place them on the table" said the Lieutenant. On the floor were six sleeping mattresses – he placed one on top of the weapons then piled the rest around the table. Next he emptied the paraffin out of the oil lamp, told us to get out, and put a match to the paraffin soaked mattresses.

We walked away quickly with our prisoners to get back to our Company and as we went down the road we could see and hear the ammunition exploding and eventually the whole building was burning. We arrived at our Camp alright and no-one was injured.

Having handed over our prisoners we all had something to eat and drink and the Officer came to thank us. That was the end of an eventful day.

It was nearly the end of April and we were on the move again, this time to re-join the other Regiments of the Brigade. A fairly large attack on Bremen was imminent and at the end of the third week in April the attack started. Our Company and X Company had to deal with an industrial area and were going to have help from some of the Dragoon Guards supported by flame-throwers.

Sadly, once again we lost our Company Commander, Captain Heatly, who had serious injuries. Our Platoon managed to squeeze down a narrow side street and put a few hand-grenades through a factory window. There were several calls to the Germans to give themselves up and eventually they walked out with their hands up. Our Company now had Major Clapham in charge. I knew him well as he had been our Signals Officer in Scotland – we found him to be a really nice guy.

It was now going into the first week in May and Bremen had been taken. I believe it was about the 3rd or 4th of May when the Company moved to an area on the southern outskirts of Bremen. I do not remember the name of it, but it was a quiet place almost like a separate little village. There was a sudden relaxing of tension in this area as no opposition could be found – but it did not stop us from keeping a look-out. German civilians still occupied their houses but kept their distance.

Around the 6th of May some of us were detailed to search the houses. We calmly went to each dwelling and explained that we had to search each home. No-one was treated badly or pushed around, although the look of fear on some of their faces suggested that was what they thought they would be experiencing; but we knew that they were finished and they were treated with a certain amount of compassion.

I went into a slightly larger farm-type house and a very elderly tired-looking man opened the door. He let me in and in the middle of the room was a middle-aged woman holding the hands of two small children. She had a tense look about her. The man showed me around the house and opened all the doors for me to look in, but as I passed back down the hallway to the front door I noticed another door which the old man seemed reluctant to open. He had a sad look on his face when I ordered him to open it. In the room was a young girl lying on a bed – she was probably about sixteen years old, but did not look very well to me. I did not disturb her and left the house. I reported this to the Officer in charge as we all had to report anything we thought suspicious. I said I was not sure if she was ill or had been punished for something. The Medical Officer who heard this said, "Show me – I'll take a look." I took him straight away and the old man let us in. The M.O. examined the girl and afterwards said to me "I believe she has T.B." He took a small bottle of tablets out of his kit of medical things and handed it to the old man and gave him instructions as to how many the girl should take per day. With a smile on the old man's face, we left.

At 6am on the 7th May, it was my turn to do a few hours in the look-out trench. It was situated on the corner of a tee-junction just up the lane and had a view in three directions. There were another two trenches each about one hundred yards from me. We had some hot tea brought to us around 8am and we expected to be relieved at 9am for breakfast. I was still on look-out at eleven o'clock when the Platoon Sergeant came over. "Jones," he said, "we have had a message come through that the war is over, but stay in the look-out until we get it confirmed." He then walked away. 'I'm sure he said the war is over' I said to myself. Later on at about one o'clock an N.C.O. came up and said, "You can come out now, Jonesy, and get some grub."

It was the 8th of May 1945. Down in the village was a sort of Community Hall. I had been in there before and there were notices in German all over the place, and photos of children. The whole of our Platoon were in there chatting and smoking. Then the cooks brought in a large dixey of stew with new bread. We got out our Mess tins and the cooks came around and gave us as much as we liked. (I had wondered for some time what had happened to those eight bloody chickens – it was chicken stew!). Not much was said about the report that had come in, but as we stuffed ourselves with the chicken stew the Platoon Officers came in and told us that it was official – the war in Europe was over. There was no rejoicing – things don't sink in as easy as that after all we'd been through. Just after the announcement, a very tall thin man in his seventies walked in; he just stood there staring at us as if he wanted to talk to us. One of the chaps who played a mouth-organ started to play 'Lili Marlene' and this old fellow started crying. Another chap asked why he was crying and told him the war was over. He told us that both his sons had gone to the Russian Front two years before and he had never heard from them. Someone else went up to him and gave him a few fags – he tried to smile then walked away.

We were told to make sure we collected everything up ready for a possible move in the morning. It was difficult to sleep that night. I think we all had similar things in our minds about the future, and was it really true the war was over?

The following morning after breakfast we all lined up in the small road in front of the houses. We had our kit, rifles etc., and as the lane we had to go along was rather narrow, we were to march out in two ranks and without further comment, it was a quiet "Forward march" from the Platoon Sergeant. As we moved out we could see some of the civilians looking out from behind their curtains. As we neared the end of the houses a woman was standing in her door-way holding a child's hand. I heard her say "Danke, danke", meaning 'thank you.' Again there was no cheering but I think we all had our own thoughts.

Thoughts came into my mind of when I first arrived at the Regiment in Lockerbie. It was late evening when the Battalion Commander greeted us all from Shrewsbury. He said, "Welcome to the finest Regiment in the Army." There were a few whispers of "The bullshit has soon started!" However, after twenty two months with the Regiment I realized he meant every word he said. I believe that what the Regiment had gone through and what it had achieved, every single man should be proud of it.

I do not think that any Infantry Commander could have expected more.

There was not a single Officer who would ask his men to do something he would not do himself. I think they were all a credit to the Regiment and to the British Army; Officers who guided the Regiment through difficult times and many who had lost their lives in doing so. I also have to say that the other two Regiments in the 185 Brigade deserve all of that recognition too, i.e. the Royal Norfolk Regiment and the Royal Warwickshire Regiment. It was not until I was much older that I was able to read of our achievements. On June 6th, D-Day, we landed around seven hundred men including our Support

Company which comprised the Carrier Platoon, the Mortar Platoon and Anti-tank Crews plus the Medical men. I discovered that on May 8th, the end of hostilities, we had six hundred and ninety six casualties – killed, wounded or missing. When Lord Montgomery named this Division his 'Ironsides' I think I can now understand what he meant.

However, this story is intended to be about me and my life, and how things were to be in later life after the hard times as a child and through the war years. When I arrived on the beaches of Normandy I suppose I felt apprehensive like most of the men but at that time I did not feel afraid even though I saw many men killed. As we moved out into the country we witnessed a soldier being blown to pieces and we had to step over his remains. Sometimes at night in our two-man dug-outs we talked about our fears and our main comment was, "I hope I get a clean bullet." By that we meant we did not want an injury where we might lose a limb, or die suffering as many did. A clean bullet meant to be killed instantly or have the sort of injury that is not serious, but enough to have us sent back home.

I was now very scared and that feeling of being scared remained with me all the while and up to the Battle of Kervenheim in Germany. There, I seemed not to think about the physical dangers. After what I had experienced, what I had done and witnessed, I wondered more about my mental state and if it would return back to normal after the war was over. I did for a while seem to lose control of myself. I insulted a tank Commander and I called him everything I could think of, as I thought he had put our lives in danger. I lost all fear as war was now part of life. As I look back now, I can only say that I did what I was able. I don't think I did any single thing that could be called brave. It may all have been a matter of circumstances at the time, but whatever it was I have no claim to be called a hero. Real heroes are few and far between, but most soldiers do what they are asked and I have witnessed them all – even our Victoria Cross man at Kervenheim who, like most V.C.s, paid with his life.

CHAPTER THIRTEEN

When we reached the main road the Troop Transporters were already waiting for us – another bit of good organisation – but where were we heading for? ('Home' we were all wishing, but we had more sense than to expect that!). I'm not sure how far we had gone when we arrived in a town that looked as if the war had passed it by. No damage was visible at all – rather difficult to understand why, considering the amount of R.A.F. attacks on Germany.

As far as I was concerned this was to be a new episode of my life – or should I say a different part of life's river, now the war was over and I probably would never have to aim my rifle at another human being again.

We disembarked in a town called Minden in the Westfarhland of Germany. It was obvious we were to Garrison the town for a while. We were dropped off on the corner of a main street and side street where there was a four storey accommodation block which had been sorted out for us in advance; in fact the building was just for our Company. After we had been allotted our rooms – two or three to a room – the Company Commander gave us some briefing regarding our duties. It was a temporary duty and we would have to patrol, search places and sometimes shut off complete streets in order to search for and catch criminals involved in Concentration Camps, as many of them had gone into hiding. We would be allowed to walk around freely providing we did not fraternise with the civilians, only talk to them in the course of our duty. Most of the time it was very peaceful, the weather was spring-like and we were comfortable in our new billets.

The main rule was that we must be in by 10pm otherwise we would be on a charge. Unfortunately I got myself into a spot of bother on this one. In my room were a couple of Cockney lads who were not very blessed with discipline, and one day they told me about a canal which was quite local. As a lad I loved going around and walking along, and sometimes fishing, the canals of Birmingham, so I asked when we could go out together for them to show me the canal system. "That's no problem" they said, "it will be very relaxing to go for a walk along the canal in the evening." So one evening after dinner we set off to the nearest path leading to the canal, and after a nice long walk, well out of the built-up area, it was suggested that we cross the next bridge to the other side as the lads assured me they knew a short cut back across the fields. Well it turned out to be a complete disaster which caused us to get back to our quarters twenty minutes late. On arrival, we saw a search party was already organised. This meant that first thing in the morning we would be on a charge. Our punishment was seven days confined to our quarters, i.e. in Army terms, seven days Jankers.

I did not realise then that it would turn out to be the best thing that had happened to me and would give me something I had always wanted in the Army. I was given a very cushy job; all I had to do was to keep the Sergeants and Regimental Sergeant Majors Mess tidy, just making sure all the chairs were back in place etc. after they had been used. This took no more than half an hour a day.

On the fifth morning, the R.S.M. came in. "Jones, you are a driver aren't you?" he asked. "Yes Sir, but I don't get chance to do much of it" I replied. He then said, "The Lieutenant needs to go on a Recce and there's no driver available. I think you had better do it." This just might be the opportunity I had been waiting for! I drove the Lieutenant about ten miles in a Company vehicle, and on the way back he asked, "Why aren't you on the M.T. Section?" "I have never been asked" was my reply. When we got back, he called over to the M.T. Sergeant and said "I want you to have this man in the M.T. Section straight away Sergeant." Well, for a long time that was what I had been waiting and hoping for, and it was through being put on seven days Jankers that it had brought me another change in my river of life – something I really wanted!

In Germany at that time there were thousands of displaced personnel, or as we called them, D.P.'s. They were all put into various camps for the authorities to sort out and get them back home as soon as possible. They were mainly Polish, French, Russian and Czechoslovakian. Most of the transportation was by the Royal Army Service Corps but owing to the work load they hadn't enough drivers. Eventually the Infantry Regiments were asked to loan out their drivers to help out. This was a great opportunity for me to do some long distance driving. I was loaned to them for three weeks and was issued with a new transporter that held about thirty personnel.

In convoys of about five transporters we had to deal with the German prisoners of war first, the idea being to get them back to the towns nearest to where they were originally from and from there to be released to their individual areas. We had to go to Hamburg, Hanover, Essen and Arnsburgh in the Ruhr Valley. Small areas of make-shift sites were laid on for overnight stops and Officers were in radio contact to tell us where to go the following morning to pick up the next load of men. It was good experience for us and in the main was enjoyable. But for the German prisoners, not so good, although they were as glad the war was over as we were. A great many of these men had not been home for a long time and were not aware of the damage that had been done to their cities and homes. When we drove into their cities, the look on their faces was a look of shock and despair and even though they were our enemies it was a job not to feel sorry for them, coming home and finding their homes were not there. (Later, my wife said "Whoever they are, they are some mothers' sons" and there is no answer to that.) We had covered a few hundred miles on the Autobahns during those three weeks and we witnessed some of the war's worst devastation which even now is very hard to forget.

When we got back to our own Station at Minden, everyone was busy – we were on the move again. I was given a Company three-ton capacity truck to drive. It looked as though the whole Battalion was off to Belgium to a place not far from Brussels – a small farming area called Eckent in the district of Haaltert. We were to travel in convoy and I was to have the Company Stores whilst towing a 6lb anti-tank gun as well. What was in all of our minds was why we were going to a quiet place in Belgium? Lots of speculation was flying around but none of us guessed the real reason.

We were eventually billeted in civilian houses with Belgian families who volunteered to have us on a short term basis. I was billeted on my own in a small farm cottage with Mr. and Mrs. Hybrech who had a twelve year old daughter named Yvonne, a family who were unbelievably kind to me and even gave me my own bedroom. All these families were paid by the Government for allowing the Army to billet their soldiers, but they were not allowed to give us any food as we had our own Mess hall in the village.

We had only been there a few days when some soldiers from another Regiment, I think they were from the Ox and Bucks Regiment, had been sent to us to make up the missing numbers. They let the cat out of the bag and said they had been told they were joining a Regiment which was going to fly from Brussels airport to America to train with the American Army to make the final assault on Japan.

About a week or ten days later, little Yvonne came running in from school shouting, "Mudder, Mudder, big bomber, big bomber bring fini!" What she had heard was that the Americans had dropped the Atom Bombs and the Japanese had surrendered. As we thought we were only going to be in Belgium for a couple of weeks, this had changed everything. As far as I was concerned it was seven weeks of little or nothing to do but enjoy ourselves. However I had a lot of other things to think about and plenty of time to do it. It was all about what to do with the rest of my life when I got home. I thought of the twenty years of my life – I'd spent them always being told or ordered what to do and I never resisted or retaliated. I thought that when I came out of the Army I wanted to be far more independent and think for myself. I did not want to be greatly ambitious but just voice my own opinions on those things I disagreed with, which I had always left to others. There was one thing I did know – since I had been on the Transport, I had gained a reputation of being handy with anything mechanical after I had been asked to help out with faults on vehicles etc. I was never after promotion nor did I ever ask for it in the Army or at work in Civvy Street.

A few times I had to take men to Brussels railway station, as some of them were well overdue for a leave and at times it made me a bit homesick but I knew that the Army had not finished with us yet. In fact new rumours were going around as to what we may be doing next.

Here in Belgium I was getting a lot of experience driving in different areas and conditions. I sometimes had to go fairly long distances although I liked what I was doing. However I had already made up my mind that it was not a job I wanted to do back home. Engineering was what I did and that was what I would end up doing. I was born in Birmingham which had earned the name of 'Workshop of the World.'

Now my River of Life was about to take another bend. It came about that the Regiment was needed in the Middle East and we were to fly out to Tripoli then on to Palestine. I found out that the British Palestine Police Force, which had been policing that area for years, was now being disbanded so our Regiment was to replace them on a temporary basis until things had settled down.

After a double journey we finally ended up just outside Jerusalem. The Regiment was positioned on a hill slightly over-looking the city. One of the comments made by the men was how great it was to be in constant warmth with plenty of sunshine – never to be soaked, lying in wet dug-outs etc. Well, we all had a shock not long after we had set up a tented Camp. During the night it chucked down snow! We could not believe our luck nor could some of the residents of Jerusalem! Most of the younger generation had never seen snow there before. It snowed the following morning too but in the late afternoon the temperature rose quickly and soon there were little rivers flowing down the hill taking with them, Mess-tins, boots and socks etc as some of the water ran right through the tents! I think the Regiment, over the past eighteen months, had had everything thrown at it but with what we had been used to, we soon recovered and were back to normal.

Our Company once again seemed to have become slightly isolated from the rest of the Battalion. We were posted a few miles away at a very small place called Ramallah. (Today it is a very large place and with the problems over the years it is well-known and in the news frequently). There was a proper Palestinian Barracks – a nice building made of stone and built by the British many years before. Y Company was to occupy this building which had proper bedrooms, two to a room; a proper dining room, its own car park, fuel store and ramps for servicing vehicles – a perfect outpost. But it was not put there just for comfort. As an outpost it always had to have a certain delegated section with transport ready for call-out at a minutes notice in case of trouble – bearing in mind the area had a history of trouble.

However, that did not stop us from providing our own entertainment. On the M.T. Section was a Corporal called Harry who was quite a character and we both seemed to go everywhere together, in fact we ran the Bingo on Saturday evenings for anyone who didn't want to go out. Any driving jobs I used to volunteer for and on many Saturday nights men wanted to go to Jerusalem for the Cafes etc. Down one of the side streets was a small Café called Ginatis. I would drop them off at Ginatis and come back to the Barracks to do the Bingo then go back down and pick them up at 10.30pm. One Saturday I must have mentioned it was my 21st birthday. When I took the chaps to Ginatis, which was a favourite place for them, they asked me to park the vehicle at the Police Station and go back to the Café. At the Café there was a three-man band comprising a violin player, an accordion player and a trumpet player who were always out of tune. When I walked in, the band started to play, "I'm 21 Today." They tried their best but we all had a good laugh! That's another night that I will always remember.

Not all nights were like that though. When there was trouble in the city we could be out on duty all night. Sometimes the lads would be out so long we had to take hot tea and food out to them. There was no real conflict between the Army and the people of that country, nor did there appear to be any real trouble between the Jews and the Arabs – it seemed to me to be just small groups of trouble-makers. There was a Jewish group called the 'Stern Gang' who always seemed to want their own way, but there was nothing like the conflict there has been between the Palestinians and Israelis of the past few years, which seems never-ending.

Whatever went on out there I wanted to enjoy the experience of being there and not for it to be like the times we had in Europe. So we had some little meetings in our own time to fix up some local trips around the area. The R.S.M. seemed to approve and eventually a guided trip around the old walled city of Jerusalem was arranged. I was surprised how many were not interested, but eventually there was a party of twenty of us. On the day we went, our C.O. gave us a little briefing. "You are going into the old city of Jerusalem and you must be on your best behaviour and show respect to the people who go there to pray. So set a good example of the British Army."

I am not a religious person, as I have previously pointed out, so at first I accepted everything with an open mind and judged by what I saw not what I had heard, but when inside the city it was unbelievably different to how I'd thought it would be. There were tiny streets and passages; tiny little shops for vegetables and clothes, and no-one seemed to be eying us up with suspicion. It gave a feeling of many years ago, as though we had gone back to the time when it was built. We were shown a large area of rock where Jesus Christ was believed to have been crucified. We were also taken into a very small stone building where there was only room for about six people. In the middle stood a statue of the Virgin Mary which was in a glass case with an open top. The open top was for offerings made by pilgrims and even in 1946 it was more than half full of jewellery. Gold rings – thousands of them – wrist bangles, necklaces etc., everything was solid gold. It makes one wonder how strong their belief and faith is and what has kept it going over the centuries.

On the same day we were taken further into the centre of Jerusalem. I had already heard of the Wailing Wall, where the Jews pray. When I had first heard of this wall as a schoolboy, it was difficult to realise and imagine people praying by it but what was so surprising, which I had been told about previously, were men and women writing little notes on tiny pieces of paper and then pushing those into the gaps between the stones. The wall is quite immense and constructed of very large stone blocks and all over the wall must have been thousands of these pieces of paper with prayers and messages. Though not religious, I can understand people wanting something to help guide them through life and for them to cling on to, but how sad that throughout history different religions will clash and even kill each other through misunderstanding and ignorance. I do not write these things to preach or to try to influence others, but we all have the right to our own opinions. As a famous man once said, "I do not agree with what you are saying, but I will fight to defend your right to say it." (Voltaire).

I am a practical person and find myself sometimes argumentative on these issues, but I really cannot understand what makes a person write little notes in the hope that 'someone' will read or hear the messages. Perhaps it's me that's entirely wrong. Perhaps it's because

I am practical and believe in what I see and feel. I do believe a lot that is written in the Bible though I think time has distorted some things. But if I have offended anyone regarding what they believe, then I apologise.

When we arrived back to our billets in Ramallah, Harry, my friend on the M.T. Section had an idea. "Ron, how about going on a Recce together to the Dead Sea. We can go on the Despatch Riders motor bike." "I think it would be better if we asked some of the others and go as a party" I remarked. "We can take ten in the Ford." A few days later we set off at about 11am. The drive there from Ramallah was all down hill except for the last couple of miles which was flat and straight. The Dead Sea is a massive inland water which is dense with salt and it was fascinating to be able to walk out of your depth and float because of that. (It all fits in with the story of Jesus walking on water!) There is a problem if you have a tender skin or if you have had a shave that morning as the salt makes you very sore, but when I was there, there were cold fresh-water showers provided for the bathers to wash off the salt. That was another experience I would not have had if I had not been in the Army. Sadly this inland sea is receding owing to man's needs.

Sometime after, a couple of months perhaps, we were on the move again. The temperature was going up and up. We stopped at a place quite near Cairo and almost as soon as we had settled I was told by the C.O. that he needed me to be his personal driver. Well, this meant a lot to me for a good many reasons. There was a great deal of driving to be done as some of the places where we set up Camp were so far from the others. The worst place I had to drive through was Cairo as it seemed every Egyptian driver had his own set of driving rules! They all drove with one hand on the horn button to warn everyone else which way they wanted to go.

In the Battalion was Major Thornycroft who commanded X Company. He was very well respected by his men because of his concern and care for them, and if there was any entertainment to be done he would join in. But for some reason he'd had to leave the Regiment while we were in Europe during the war. One day I had to take our Major Clapham into Cairo for a meeting with other Officers. I had to stop outside a small hotel and Major Clapham went inside. "I won't be long" he said, so I sat in the Jeep reading a Service Manual. Suddenly a very tall Officer came out and strode straight over to me. I recognised him straight away – it was Major Thornycroft whom I hadn't seen for about fifteen months. He got into the Jeep and shook my hand. "I haven't seen a Private of the Regiment for ages as I have been away for some time. I thought I would take this opportunity to come and see you" he said. It was typical of the man to do that, and he wished me luck then went back into the meeting.

In June 1983 I went to Normandy for a two-week stay. I met both Major Clapham and Major Thornycroft over there, right where our Front Line trenches had been on the night of D-Day. They asked my wife and me to have a drink with them. Major Thornycroft even remembered that day in Cairo where we had met up again. I also knew that they were very close friends and both had reached the rank of Colonel. It was very nice talking to two such really good men – a time I will always remember.

But to get back to the story – I was still in Egypt. We had been to many places: Suez, Haifa, El Quassasin, and seen the Pyramids – what more could I have wanted.

There had been no conflict for us to deal with although we did some spells of patrols along the Suez Canal, but apart from the discomfort of the heat we had little or no trouble. The time there seemed to go quickly and then it looked as if we were on the move again to do some duties in Cyprus. This time we found out what we were going there for. I rather felt I could look forward to that and the country itself as it would also give me a wider experience of people and the world we live in. I had the feeling it may be the last place my Army life would take me as I knew my demob time couldn't be too far away.

CHAPTER FOURTEEN

About that time many Jewish people were leaving German and other European countries, and were commandeering ships from the Germans or using any other means of transport to get to Palestine. This had been going on for a while but the British Navy was diverting them into Cyprus as these people were classed as illegal immigrants. Also, there was the possibility of Germans from the S.S. or Concentration Camp guards trying to escape by pretending to be Jews.

In Cyprus a large camp had been set up to house these people whilst being interrogated etc before they could be released. When we arrived there, a camp was already prepared for us a short distance from the Holding Camp. There were rows of tin huts which were fairly comfortable. The nearest little town was Famagusta, a pleasant little fishing village right on the coast, which even had a café for British troops and quite a few good little drinking places.

When we had settled down, I drove the Commander around the perimeter of the Holding Camp which had a main gate with a Guard already in position. There were four look-out towers about twenty feet high, complete with search lights for night time use. Our soldiers would be taking it in turn to be in those look-outs in shifts over twenty four hours each day. Although we had a lot to do, we also had enough free time to ourselves. There was a fair sized Parade Ground situated in the middle of the rows of huts if we needed to be kept occupied, and the small town of Famagusta was only about four miles from the Camp.

After about a week we were well organized. I had already done quite a bit of driving. On two occasions the Commander and two others had to be driven to Nicosia, the capital, for meetings with Commanders of other Regiments. I also acquired the job of taking the lads into Famagusta on Saturday evenings (which I had volunteered for) so I couldn't complain. The vehicle soon got the nickname 'The Passion Wagon' – I wonder why! My bunk was the first one near the door of the hut so that a quick message could be given to me. Many an evening a young Second Lieutenant who I knew well, would pop his head around the door and ask if I could run them into the town. There was another Lieutenant who I was getting to know who had not been with us for long – he was a regular caller. However I would never let anyone use the Commander's vehicle unless I knew he had gone out for the evening with another Officer, using another vehicle.

One day Peter Potter came in to see me. He was the chap who joined us as a Reserve the night we crossed the Rhine. "Hello Ron" he said, "I've been trying to contact you for some time. I heard you eventually got the job of driving the Commander around." "Well Peter, I wondered where you had got to. A lot of changes have taken place since I first met you – lots of new faces since the War, and many of the older chaps have been demobbed." Peter agreed. "Have you been into Famagusta yet?" I asked him. "No" he replied. "Right, let's go tomorrow night. I have nothing else to do so we will take the Jeep." "Is that alright?" he asked. "Yes, I have the O.K. to use it if I want to go into town." Peter was highly delighted as he had not been out since we came to Cyprus, and he was not the pushy sort.

The following night as usual, a couple of Second Lieutenants wanted a lift into town. I thought Peter would be a bit surprised when he showed up. I told the Officers I would pick them up near their Quarters, so that Peter would not know. I knew Peter would be the soul of discretion and with his polite and understanding manner he could talk to anyone. Peter arrived looking forward to the little trip out. "I know a nice little café where you can get a pork chop, chips and fried egg for 2/6d and wine if you want it" I told him. "I can't wait!" he said. "Just a minute, though" I said, "I have to pick up a couple of my friends." I pulled up outside the Officers Quarters and the two young Officers jumped into the back of the Jeep. "Thanks Jones, drop us outside the café where they have the dance floor." I knew exactly where it was. Off we went, with Peter in the front seat probably wondering what to say, but I couldn't see the expression on his face as it was quite dark and there were hardly any lights on the road. I told him to look out for bats as they were usually about at that time of night and flying from tree to tree. I explained how one once actually fell into the Jeep one night!

When I dropped the two young Officers off they offered me ten shillings to go for a drink, but I always refused when I was offered a few shillings. "No thanks Sir, we are O.K. and I mustn't drink too much when driving – but thanks all the same."

"O.K. for 10.30 to pick us up?" they asked. "Yes, that's fine" I agreed, and we went on our way. "You old bugger!" said Peter, "I did not expect that!" "Wait till we get to the café and I will explain" I said. I think Peter was surprised at the quality of the meal we ordered – pork chops, fried eggs and chips – which was quite a change from the Army food and sitting in the Mess Hall eating it.

I thought I had better explain to Peter about giving lifts to the younger Officers. "Yes Pete, I do give lifts to the younger Officers when it's possible, but I do have permission to do this and I can refuse. I know in the British Army it's frowned upon for Officers and men to associate with each other in our free time, as it may cause a loss of discipline. An Army without discipline is a lost Army." Peter really understood all this although he had not been in the Army long, but he did not lack intelligence. I also reminded him that whatever they discussed together was never repeated by me or their batmen, and that although they appreciated the lifts they would soon tell us if they were not happy with what we may say or do, and that's how it had to be.

I had a long chat with Peter and found him to be a good listener. I explained to him that I was never an ambitious person and would never ask for promotion, but when I was back in Civvy Street I wanted something a little better than just working in a factory and although I was not a very technical person, I made up for it with my practical ways. Peter had had a very good education and understood what I was trying to get over. He then carefully quoted something to me. He said a famous man once said, "Every man sometime in his life experiences twenty minutes of glory which often gives him confidence to exploit his gifts." That was another little thing I have always remembered.

It was nearly ten-thirty and I reminded him we had better go. We picked up the two Officers on time and one of them asked, "Had a nice time?" "Yes, very enjoyable" said Peter. We arrived back to our Barracks feeling very contented – another day gone.

Over the next week things were quiet and uneventful. Then something interesting happened – well for me anyway. There was a brick building about fifteen foot square which housed the generator which powered both our Camp and the Holding Camp. I had never been inside it, but one night I had the opportunity to do so by sheer coincidence. About half a mile down the road was an open air cinema which had not been used since we arrived, but someone had managed to get it up and running with a black and white film called "Tall in the Saddle" starring John Wayne. Those who were off duty could go, and it was free. The cinema had four walls, a door and a pile of seats which you could put wherever you wanted to sit. Having no roof, you could watch the stars when the film wasn't on.

After the film had been running for about half an hour, suddenly the projector started to go slow and it eventually stopped as all the power had gone. There was some laughing, some booing, and everyone lit matches for fun. After a short while an Officer in a Jeep pulled up outside and promptly walked to the front of the cinema and shouted, "Anyone here know anything about diesel engines?" I was amazed when several chaps called out, "Jones over here Sir." He came to me and asked, "Can you fix the diesel engine for us?" "I know nothing about diesel engines, Sir" I said. "Do you know anything about engines at all?" he demanded. "Yes Sir, but only petrol engines." "Right, come with me" he said. I could have murdered those who called out my name! We went to the generator room and inside were three or four N.C.O.'s holding candles and one Officer shining a torch for a Cypriot chap who was on the floor taking things to pieces. "That's not a diesel engine Sir" I pointed out, "it's a Ford V8 petrol engine." "Can you fix it?" he quickly asked. "I'll do my best Sir" I replied.

Well, I knew that I had to act positively now that I had an audience around me. I was a bit nervous knowing the situation they had put me in, as all the Camp power had gone. "Out of the way" I said to this Cypriot chap, "let's see what you've done." He had the carburettor in pieces on a sheet of paper – I examined it and told him "There's nothing wrong with that" so I re-assembled it as quickly as I could and bolted it back into the engine. "I will test the ignition first by taking out a spark-plug" I said to the Cypriot, though I don't think he knew what I was talking about. I removed the first spark-plug and immediately spotted the trouble. I removed two more plugs to make sure and on all of them the electrodes were burned away. The engine had never been serviced properly. "I'll need eight new spark-plugs" I said to the Officer. "Sergeant, go and get the man the spark-plugs from the M.T. Stores." "The M.T. Stores will be locked up now Sir" he replied. "Then break the blasted door down! This is an emergency!" Within a few minutes the Sergeant came back with a box of new plugs. I had removed all eight plugs while he was away and it took about another ten minutes to fix the new ones in place, and although the Cypriot chap was objecting as he wanted to do it, I grabbed the starting handle, gave it a couple of swings and the engine started – and we heard a lot of cheering from around the Camp!

"Thank you Jones" said the Officer, "get into the Jeep and I will run you back to the cinema." As he dropped me off he thanked me again, but I could tell he was very angry as the most important engine in the Camp was not being maintained and it was obvious to me he was going to jump on someone when he got back! As I walked into the cinema the film was just starting to run again, and I got a rousing cheer! I wondered if that was what Peter meant when he said that every man has twenty minutes of glory in his life!

CHAPTER FIFTEEN

During the next few days, something happened to change the rest of my life – and for the good I might add! The Company Commander's batman, a chap called Lewis who came from Birmingham and who I'd known for a very long time, called to see me one evening as he'd done many times before. "Ron, I have a niece who lives not too far from me who looks after her young sister and her father as her mother is very poorly, and as I know you don't write to any girls like most of the chaps do, I wondered if you would like to write to her as a pen-pal?" "Oh, I don't know about that – I used to write to a girl and unknown to me she was knocking about with a bloody Yank. In fact she married him while I was in Scotland. It put me off girls." I replied. "No, she's not like that, she's a very honest girl" said Lewis. "Well, alright then – I'll write on Saturday evening if I'm not too busy" I said. He gave me her address and left.

A few days later something else happened. The second in command of the Company came over while I was cleaning the Jeep. "You will be driving a new C.O. next week. Major Clapham is going back to England at the weekend for some training for a different command job." "Do we know the new one?" I asked. "Only that he has been in charge of an Indian Regiment and his name is Busby and he will be bringing his wife with him, so you may find yourself quite busy." When the second in command left, I suddenly thought of something. When I was at work in Civvy Street, I knew a chap named Busby who told me of a relation of his who ran away from home and joined the Army as a boy soldier, and ended up in India as an Officer. No, I thought, it could not be such a coincidence as to be the same man.

Over the next few days I was kept quite busy as Major Clapham had a lot to do before he left. On the Sunday morning I had to take him to catch his ship home. We both wished each other well and said goodbye. I felt a bit sad at the time as I had first met Major Clapham in Scotland when he was Signals Officer and I was put on a course after I had tried so hard to get off it by deliberately making spelling mistakes etc on the test sheet! I didn't see Major Clapham again until 1983 when I went to Normandy with my wife. We immediately recognised each other even after 39 years.

With what had been going on, I had forgotten to write to my friend's niece and it was Sunday evening when I saw Lewis coming over to see me again. "I'm just going to write that letter, as I was too busy to do it last night," I told him, "I'll put in a small photo of myself as well." The Welsh chap in the bunk opposite remarked, "That will put the woman off straight away, Boyo!" A little bit of bad language came from me at that remark! "O.K." said Lewis, "let me know when you hear from her. I'll have to get back now as I have to get things ready for the new C.O."

A couple of days later, I heard that the new Commander had arrived at the Camp and was busy being introduced to the rest of the Officers and shown around the Camp. At about five o'clock I was sent for to take him to the small place where he would be staying with his wife in Famagusta. I waited outside his office for a few minutes, then the second in command came out with the Major. "This is Jones, your driver" he said. Within a few minutes we were off to Famagusta, and the Major asked me how long I had been with the Regiment. "Ever since I joined up in early 1943, Sir" I told him. I knew exactly where he was staying and stopped right outside his place. I made no comment as I could see he was very tired after all his travelling. "I would like you to pick me up at eight o'clock in the morning, please Jones" he said.

I picked him up on time the next morning and his wife waved him off. On the way back to Camp he again asked me a few questions about myself and the Company. He seemed to have a very friendly attitude – nothing aloof about him at all, so I felt quite at ease with him. I didn't see him during the day, but took him back home at 5.30. He commented that his wife had probably been getting used to the area and finding out where the shops etc were. I mentioned that the R.S.M.'s wife was living only a couple of hundred yards from their place. He'd been told that, and asked me to show him where it was. I did this and he seemed quite pleased. I dropped him off at his home and returned to the Barracks.

A couple of weeks later, Lewis came to see me. "Have you heard from Joan?" he asked. "No, it's a bit soon isn't it?" I said. "Well, I've just received a letter from home" he told me, "and I've had bad news. Joan's mother has died – so don't write to her again until I hear more." "No of course not – I'm really very sorry to hear that, so I'll wait until I hear from you. Joan will really have her hands full now."

One morning I was bringing Major Busby back to Camp when he asked, "Are the men in the Company happy about everything; do they have things to grumble about?" "Not really, Sir, they all seem to be happy about being in Cyprus – probably better here than most places where we've been stationed. There's only one thing I hear them often asking; some time ago when the system came in about giving soldiers so many stars according to their experience etc which may affect their pay, they did their exam for it but have never heard anything since." The Major made a note of that and within a couple of weeks every soldier had his star ranking. I was given the full four stars – I believe it was for bringing it to his attention.

Major Busby and his wife were keen on seeing more of the island in their spare time and as I drove for them I had chance to see places too. The Major used to like to find nice beaches with another Officer and his wife, and spend some time picnicking at these places.

During this time I received a very nice letter from Joan to which I replied straight away as obviously she was in a sad state losing her mother so young. From then on we corresponded regularly and I started to look forward to her letters which were all nicely written with none of the sloppy comments that some of the lads' girls wrote!

One day while I was taking the Major back to his billet, he mentioned that he had joined the Army as a boy soldier at sixteen years of age, and ended up in an Indian Regiment. This immediately reminded me of the chap I had worked with before the war whose name was Busby and who had told me about his relation who'd joined the Army at sixteen, so I told Major Busby about that and he was quite surprised. "What was his name and what was he like?" he asked. "Well," I replied, "his name was Busby, same as yours, and we called him Bill. He was about my height with blond curly hair." "Well I'll be blowed, that sounds like young Bill, if he worked in a factory!" When we got to his temporary home he invited me in then proceeded to tell his wife I had worked with his relation. "What a coincidence!" she remarked, then she asked if I would like a cup of tea. "Yes, thank you, I am a bit thirsty" I said. Like the Major, his wife was very nice to talk to – nothing aloof about either of them. She told me she had served as a WREN during the war days. After a nice long chat I said, "I will have to go now to do some servicing on the transport." I did not want to overstay my welcome and I left for the Barracks.

It was now early 1947. I knew my demob. would not be long and was already thinking of what I wanted to do. I was getting regular letters from my mother and father, and I had written to them about the nice girl, Joan, I was writing to and I had asked Joan to go and see my parents if she wanted to. My Dad wrote back to me approving of the suggestion, also remarking how bad the weather was back in England. He explained about the long winter and the snow coming up to the bottom of the windows in places! I could hardly imagine it out there in Cyprus in the lovely climate!

We had recently had one very bad accident when we had a heavy rainfall, the worst we'd had since being in Cyprus. Sadly one of the chaps in the look-out tower was electrocuted because of a fault on the search light. He was given a full Military funeral by the Regiment and was laid to rest in Cyprus. I'm only sorry I cannot remember his name.

I continued to be very busy with my job. Major Busby was frequently sending for me and working hard himself to keep the Company organized. I got to know the man very well and he and his wife seemed to appreciate all I did.

I was now writing often to my pen-pal Joan, and she to me. It was strange I hadn't met her but I was somehow getting to know what she was like through her pleasant and honest letters, and was looking forward to seeing her one day. It was nearly Spring and I had another letter from home telling me the snow and ice was starting to thaw.

One afternoon Major Busby sent for me but he did not want the use of the transport, so I walked over to his office and as always, knocked on his door. "Come in" he called. I walked in and saluted. He was studying some paperwork. "The Adjutant reminded me you are due to leave us in a few weeks for your demob." "Yes Sir, I believe it is soon" I answered. "Well I am sorry you are leaving but I wondered if you would consider what I am going to offer you. If you sign on for another few years I will guarantee that you will be with me as my driver all that time, and I will make you up to Sergeant Driver." He sat quietly looking at me. I thought for a moment and thanked him for his suggestion, but I knew I had to be straight and honest with him, as he had always been with me. "I am very sorry, Sir, but I wish to take my demob. so cannot accept your offer." He clearly understood, and said, "Alright, but I am sorry you are leaving us. O.K. that's all." I walked out of his office and felt very sad to have to say 'no' to such a nice man. Three days later someone else took over my job and two weeks after that I had to get ready to leave with the rest of the lads being demobbed.

The day before we left I met up with Major Busby who made the gesture of coming over to see me to wish me luck – then the day we were to embark, Peter, the young chap who spent his first battle experience in the Dug-out with me on the Rhine, came over especially to wish me well. Sadly I have never seen him since.

CHAPTER SIXTEEN

We set sail in an old converted liner named the Dunata Castle, an old cruise ship now used as a troop carrier, heading for Liverpool. The first few days were really pleasant going through the Mediterranean Sea and stopping off at Malta to pick up more passengers. But things changed when we passed Gibraltar and sailed north up to the Bay of Biscay, an area well known for its high seas. When we were half way across it seemed everyone was being sea-sick. I felt fine until a patrolling Sergeant came up to me and said, "You look as though you are O.K. on your feet, follow me." He took me into the block of men's toilets, handed me a broom and bucket and ordered me to help clean up the mess. I think I was only in there for about five minutes before I too was hanging my head over the side!

The day after, we entered calmer waters. I'm not sure but I think it took about seven days from Cyprus until we were sailing up the Clyde and into Glasgow. After disembarking we stayed overnight at a Camp and from there, the following morning, we were taken by rail to a Holding Camp a few miles from Shrewsbury in Shropshire, where we stayed until our actual demob. which was to be four or five weeks later. The Camp was very comfortable; there were no Parades – just meal times, and we were free to go home for six days leave after we had been there a few days. We did have an occasional roll-call – but who would want to abscond with only a few weeks to go!

Whilst there I met my friend Harry who had been on the M.T. Section with me when we were in Palestine. He was always good fun to be with and we both looked forward to the first week at home. I wrote home to let them know I would be back at the weekend and I also wrote to Joan to tell her I would come to see her on the Monday. But how to approach a girl I had never seen before? Some would say to take a bunch of flowers – however, I would wait until I got home and ask my sisters!

Friday mid-day seemed to be a long way off but it soon came and after lunch we collected our passes and scrounged a lift to the station. When on the train I said to Harry, "It feels very strange sitting here in freedom; almost a twinge of nervousness." "I'm going to make the most of it" Harry replied. Harry's parents had a small shop and he gave me the details where it was. "Next week I'll come over to see you" I promised. I felt that the week was going to be important to me, meeting a girl I hadn't yet seen, and thought perhaps it might just be the once only. Though if she was anything like the way she wrote I was sure we would get on – but I had no great plans as yet.

When we arrived at Birmingham New Street station, that old familiar smell made us feel really at home! "Have a good time Harry, I'll try and get to see you" I said. It was about 5.30pm when I walked into the house and was greeted by my mother and young sister. My two older sisters were now married and my father hadn't arrived home yet. I flopped down in the armchair and I don't think I moved out of it for some time, just trying to take in the fact that it had been nearly four and a half years since I first left for the Army and remembering all that had happened in between.

My father eventually came in and I thought he looked much older. He'd had his worries too, after all, both his sons had been in theatres of war and his son-in-law was in the Parachute Regiment and had been wounded at Arnhem, taken prisoner and was reported missing for four months. So I could understand his quietness and feelings at my home-coming. When I saw my older sister she told me that my Mom had prayed every night for us while the war was on.

We stopped in that night and talked and talked, though my father did not talk about the war – he'd seen more than enough in the First World War. At seventeen and a half he was with the Infantry on the Somme where most of his Regiment were lost. I think I understood him better then than I had ever done before. Although I had seen enough, it could never have been as bad as his times in the Front Line. My mother and father were good, kindly people even through their hard times, so I have always considered myself to be very lucky.

"Do you know what you want to do when you get your demob" asked my Dad. "Well the first thing I am going to do is buy myself a motorbike" I told him. Straight away I could see my mother's worried look. "They're bloody death traps those bikes" she said. "Don't worry, Mom, I may change my mind" I replied quickly, "Let's have a drink." So Dad brought out the two bottles of beer he had bought for that evening. After a glass of beer, my mother reminded me, "Joan came to see us a few weeks ago; she's a nice girl" she said. "Yes, but there's nothing serious you know – we have only been writing to each other" I replied, "but I'm looking forward to meeting her."

The weekend went well, trying to catch up with the past. On Saturday morning I went round to see if any of the lads at the old factory were still there. I met Bill Busby who had told me about his uncle joining the Army as a boy soldier and becoming a Major. I was able to tell him that his uncle had become our Company Commander and I had been his driver. He stood there in disbelief. "What a coincidence! Wait 'till I tell my wife!" he said in total surprise. The rest of the day I walked around Birmingham and visited the old Bull Ring which held a lot of memories for me. Sunday was very much the same, visiting relations and friends and going out with my father for a drink.

Monday was going to be a big day for me and I was really looking forward to seeing the girl I had been writing to for six months. She lived about ten miles away and her house was a prefabricated one, which many people had been given, as so many houses had been destroyed during the bombing of the city. So it was going to be a couple of bus rides for me, but that was no problem as I knew exactly where it was. I couldn't find a flower shop – there weren't many about those days in 1947, but I passed a Green-grocers shop and the only interesting thing they had were cherries, so I bought her a bag; not very appropriate I know!

Joan must have seen me pass the window as when I rang the bell she called "Come in." She was sitting on the settee smoking a cigarette which looked about six inches long. "Hello, nice to meet you" was the only thing I could think of saying, and as she replied she started to cough. "Would you like a cigarette?" she tried to say without coughing. When I looked at them I saw they were an expensive type called 'Markovich' and they had black tips on the ends. "I'm sorry" Joan said, still coughing, "I don't really smoke" (In fact I've never seen her smoke again!) I didn't say anything as it was obvious she also was a little nervous and was trying to smoke to impress me! However we soon settled down to normal conversation after a cup of tea and the more we talked the more I realised Joan was a very uncomplaining person. She also had experienced a lot of hard times and all this had been reflected in her letters. She was looking after her young sister who was still at school, and her father who was a truck driver for a furniture firm. It was obvious to me they were not very well off and yet were very quiet and appreciative.

I saw Joan a number of times that week and I also met her father who was a big man and like his daughter, was very easy to get on with. I could now see why she was like she was. It was soon apparent that Joan was going to be more than a pen-friend and it seemed as though she realised that too and accepted me as her boyfriend. (Over the years I have often reminded her about the day we first met and the cigarette she was trying to smoke!) We arranged to go out with Harry and his girlfriend before I had to go back to the Camp. Harry was always good fun. However I was in a more serious mood as I was thinking more about my future as I would soon be home for good, but I'd enjoyed the week knowing that I could come home every weekend until my demob.

Towards the weekend, Harry's mother had bought him an old 1934 Rover car as a present. It became our transport for our weekend leaves. The car was continually going wrong but it created a lot of fun. It was the only private car at the Camp and was kept parked alongside our Hut – which did not go down very well with the Adjutant!

I saw Joan each weekend and learned more about her. She was a very calm person and seemed happy to go along with any arrangement I made. She was also kind and tolerant, which in a way suggested that at times there may be a problem as I had learned a lot about myself over the years and knew I could be a moody sod and a very impatient person, and probably a bit dominant – things I had not realised when I was younger. I'd never had a lot of money or had any ambition to be rich, but I didn't like mean people. Fortunately Joan was extremely good natured I found, so no problem there!

One Thursday it was announced that about thirty of us would be leaving the next day for our demob. We were to be transported to a place just outside Liverpool to get our final briefing, and later in the morning we would be taken to a building in Liverpool, near to the railway station. Here we would pick up our final pay packet, be issued with a railway pass for home, collect a supply of civilian clothes then catch a train home.

Sadly, and very upsetting for all of us, as we were being driven to the place by the station, the truck in front was in collision with a tramcar. One of the men was thrown out of the truck and was killed. A tragedy on the day of his demob – a man who had served with us in Germany and Holland – a man who within the next hour would have been on the train and on his way home.

We were all silent as we went into the building to collect our final belongings. As we walked in we saw rows of blue pin-striped suits hanging up. "Sort out a suit of the size you want, also a hat and a pair of shoes then I'll stamp your railway warrants" said the man in charge. We were allowed to keep our Army Battledress, boots and Great-coats along with our kit-bags. "Is that the only colour suit you have?" I asked. "Yes Mate" was the reply. "It seems the authorities want to clone all ex-servicemen" I told him, as I had seen this brand of suit many times. I walked along with the others but as I ventured a bit further than the rest, I found a door behind a row of suits and as it was unlocked I had a look inside. It was a small room and hanging up I saw a row of good quality tweed herring-bone style suits and found one a perfect fit for me! I told some of the other lads about those suits. As I handed it to a checker on the door, he gave me a funny look. "Stamp my railway warrant, Mate" I said.

All complete, I walked out to the railway station and sat on my kit bag waiting for the train with a couple of the lads also going to Birmingham. We sat talking and commiserating about the poor chap who had been killed. We felt very sorry for his family who would be waiting for his return. I will never forget that.

The train came in, but I don't remember much about the journey home. When I arrived at New Street Station, my sister and brother-in-law were waiting for me. "Welcome home, Ron, great to see you back!"

CHAPTER SEVENTEEN

As I had already had a full week's leave and a number of weekend passes, I soon quickly settled down to home life. I had decided I wanted to continue seeing Joan and she also was happy about that. I purchased a motorbike, as I'd promised myself, and I went out quite a lot taking Joan with me and generally enjoying myself sight-seeing. My mind was quite oblivious to everything else.

After about five weeks my mother quietly said to me while I was having my lunch, "Don't you think you should start work soon?" I had a horrible feeling of guilt that I was letting my parents keep me and that I wasn't bringing any money home. "Yes, Mom, I will go and look for a job; probably go to my old factory and see if they have any vacancies." The following day I walked to my old firm but a couple of hundred yards before I got there I saw a notice, 'Engineers Wanted' on the door of another small factory. I rang the bell and a chap wearing a light brown overall came out. "You have some vacancies" I remarked. "Yes, what do you do?" he asked. "I've just come out of the Army, but I used to work at the factory up the street, tool making until I was called up" I told him. "No problem" he said, "can you start on Monday at eight o'clock?" "That's fine" I replied, and gave him my name and address. As soon as I told my mother, I think she gave a sigh of relief and went straight out to buy me some overalls.

The following Monday I walked into the factory at 7.45am and I think I was the first of the workers. At the end of the day I had decided that this was no good for me; it was a dull, boring little place. Whilst in the Army I had made up my mind that I wanted a job with interest, so on the Wednesday at mid-day I took a walk up to the factory where I had been previously employed and asked them if they had vacancies. "Of course we have; we would be glad to have you back" said the old

Manager. I went straight back and with an apology, handed in my notice after only two and a half days. I went home after they had given me the bit of pay they owed me, gave my mother the cash and told her what I had done. "Don't worry though Mom, I'm starting at my old place on Monday" I told her. She knew I was having trouble settling because so much had changed. I decided to get my motorbike out and go straight over to see Joan. I spent most of the time I had just gadding about and seeing Joan. I found her to be a very agreeable person and very pleasant.

However I knew I had to get to grips with employment and I started on the Monday as arranged. Things again were so much different at the factory to how it was when I first worked there. The products had changed and lots of women were employed there now, operating the production machines. I tried to brush aside everything I did not like. The work was easier but most of the older men I knew had gone. But I had to start earning to get some money into the bank and to give Mom a regular weekly amount. There did not seem to be anything cheerful about the place now – everyone had their heads down. The firm had been on war work while I was away and the atmosphere was as though the damned war was still on! After I had been there about six weeks I had already made up my mind I was not going to stop there. I did not say anything to my mother – she had done enough worrying over me.

About four hundred yards from where I lived was a factory, and as a small boy I was fascinated by the large machinery they had which could easily be seen when the big gates were open. They manufactured tyre moulds and heavy Vulcanizing machines. Some of the lathes were big enough to swing eight foot diameter castings weighing up to three or four tons. One Saturday morning I saw the Foreman standing outside. I knew who he was as he had chased me off the premises a few times when I was a kid. I wandered over to him; "Good morning" I said, "things haven't changed a bit around here. I've been in the Army for some time." "Yes I know – I remember you when you were at school." "Really" I said. "Yes, you were a cheeky little bugger!" he remarked with a smile. So I plucked up my courage and asked "Have you any vacancies? I have always worked in engineering." "Can you do die-sinking and pattern-cutting and engraving?" he asked. "Yes, no problem – right up my street" I said. "Can you start on Monday week?"

"Yes, thanks, I'll see you then" I replied. I felt quite relieved as over the past few weeks I sensed my river of life had got me up a creek without a paddle. But now I needed to make more of an effort.

So on Monday, back at the old firm, I told the Foreman I was giving my notice in and wanted to leave the next Friday. He understood, and said "There are a lot of chaps like you who can't settle when they first come out of the Forces." I apologised for any inconvenience I might have caused. "I'll get your money and cards sorted out for Friday" he said, and wished me luck.

The following Monday I started my new job. They put me on machining the patterns in tyre moulds and I was expected to make and grind my own milling cutters. I was on my own doing this job which suited me fine. More and more types of jobs were expected of me but I seemed to cope alright and it was far more interesting than at the other two factories. After about twelve months I had settled in and had saved a bit of money.

One Saturday afternoon I drove over to see Joan and stayed there quite late. I asked her if she would marry me. "Of course I will, but you will have to ask my father as I am not twenty-one yet" she reminded me. In those days it was right and proper to approach a lady's father first for his approval. I waited until eleven o'clock for him to come home. He was an easy man to talk to so I was not too worried. "I hope you don't mind me being here this late" I said. "I have asked Joan to marry me and she reminded me I should ask you first for your approval. I had his approval straight away, so a lot of arrangements now had to be made – the first thing was to tell my parents. The news went down well with them as they both liked Joan.

We arranged the wedding for February 1949, to be held at St.Lawrence Church in Northfield. We hadn't a great deal of money to spend on the wedding and Joan made her own wedding gown. She made a great job of it and looked really lovely on the day. As Joan was still looking after her young sister and father, it was agreed I was to move in with them.

Everything was going very well, but I wanted to do better at work. During late summer, Joan told me she was pregnant which of course would change things. I sold my motorbike and bought a 1932 Standard car for £75. There was no M.O.T. in those days, so to go out with bald tyres was not unusual – in fact you could see the canvas showing through the rubber of two of the tyres!

Soon after our son David was born, we took my mother and father to Wales for a day out. As we went up the Horseshoe Pass, the clutch started slipping so I had to do some road-side adjustment which luckily got us home. I think my parents were glad I had plenty of vehicle repair experience to get us back in that old car!

Things got better for me back at work. The factory was in a very old building, but about four hundred yards away, they had a much more modern factory and I was given the job of tool-making there. It meant I was the only toolmaker in the building and had to make and supply tools for all the workers in there. This was quite a challenge but I revelled in taking it on.

As I was earning a little more money, I got rid of the Standard car and bought a 1934 Morris at an auction. It was a much bigger car and more suitable for our needs, as shortly afterwards we had our second son, Robert, and as we felt we should move out of Joan's father's house we took the plunge and invested our money in a two-bedroom house with a nice long back garden. Joan, I felt, was happier now we had our own home. It cost the princely sum of £1,500 and my parents had given us the deposit of £150.

Back at work, a new Pantograph machine with multiple ratios was required for our Department. The designs were complete and I was given the job of building it. I was now doing exactly what I wanted to do which tested my practical skills. It took something like nine months to complete and was immediately put to work.

By this time Joan had given birth to our daughter Valerie. We were happy to have a daughter and our family was now complete. We decided that we did not want our children to be cared for by anyone else. Joan had already given up her little job and with her loving care, any financial problems would take care of themselves.

I had now been at this factory for about eight years and it had given me a chance to boost my confidence. I had a lot to do with heavy machinery there and intricate master patterns for the engravers etc. But now I felt I needed to move on. I was never an ambitious person for promotion – I just wanted work that I could get involved with and enjoy doing.

I saw an advertisement for a toolmaker. It sounded interesting and was much nearer home which would cut the travelling by half. That also appealed to me so I phoned about the position and I was requested by letter to go for an interview. After a bit of a grilling by the Tool-room Manager, I was given the job. "I suppose you will have to give a weeks notice to your present firm?" he asked. "Yes it's only right I do that" I said. "Then can you start on the following Monday?" "Certainly" I replied. On the way home my head was spinning, thinking about the questions he had asked and realising it would be a big move for me. This was going to be the most modern factory I had worked in.

After I had been there for about six months doing every day tool making, and servicing production tools, I was asked to do development work making prototypes of new products. This meant that I had to use all the various types of machines in the tool department to achieve the making of those components. It was at times very trying and I only had sketches to work from – but it suited me.

After about twelve months the Tool-room Foreman left to work at Joseph Lucas. The Chargehand took his job over and I was asked to take over as Chargehand. I felt a bit embarrassed by this as I had only been there a short time and the other chaps had been there for several years – but they did not seem to mind and we all got on with the new changes.

I had always though that a person with a job needing a lot of concentration should have a hobby or interest to take away any possible stress and have a complete change. I joined the nearest Gliding Club – something I had always wanted to do, and it would not interfere with my work though I did not realise how much I would get involved.

Back at work things began to change and also change my life. The tool-room Foreman was going to take a position at a training college to teach engineering, so I was offered the post of Foreman which I knew was a big responsibility, being in charge of skilled men. The firm had become a member of an association called the Birmingham Productivity Association. This meant that every month two Managers and I would have to visit other factories to see if we could find anything that could be altered to enhance their productivity. They in turn would visit our factory and offer the same service. Each visit would last a whole day.

Sometimes we would spot things that could speed up a production line or enable some jobs to be done to save money. The main thing was, it was enhancing my own engineering experience.

Once, a group of twenty eight of us were flown to Edinburgh to go round the Ferranti factory. They were manufacturing guided missiles for warfare. I was shown the advancement in tool-room machines, operated and controlled by computer. Everything was of high technology and it gave us all plenty to think about.

I had been with the firm some twelve years and the work load was piling up. I was looking after the apprentices and had also acquired the job of Safety Officer. Although I was enjoying most of it, my health was suffering. Then one weekend at home, I had a minor heart attack and was off work for a month. But it gave me time to think about everything, and to evaluate where I was going wrong. The first thing was to give up the Gliding Club. I was in a syndicate of four and I had achieved Bronze and Silver Certificates of which I was very satisfied. When I really thought hard about it, I realized I had been selfish going to the Gliding Club so often at weekends. Joan, all this time, continued working hard looking after the family so well and accepting what I did. I knew I needed to make a few changes so any hobby or interests I took up would have to be ones I could do at home.

I returned to work after a month's recuperation. The owner of the factory had been over to the U.S.A. to find out about a new method of production known as Cold Impact Extrusion – or just Cold Extrusion. I knew that this would deeply involve me, being in charge of the tool-room. In the meantime I tried to spend more time with the family by having a few holidays by the sea. We occasionally drove down to Weston-Super-Mare or Burnham by the Sea for a day out with the children, and those days were enjoyed by us all.

Back at work, large presses were being installed for the new type of work. Presses up to six hundred tons capacity were needed for this new process and I was getting more and more involved in the development. I believe we were very successful considering we were not a large firm. Many other firms in the country were trying to develop this method but were not successful. I attended many conferences organised in the U.K. to discuss the problems and successes.

Joan continued as usual to work hard looking after the children and me, while I was getting involved in my new hobby of restoring vintage radios, but I eventually gave that up as it was taking up too much of my time! I was now forty seven years old. In the family there was a cause for concern as my eldest sister had been diagnosed with advanced cancer.

CHAPTER EIGHTEEN

Things were hotting up at the factory and most of the time the new process was in full swing, but it was becoming very expensive. The tools needed a more technical approach and the production needed practical engineering improvement. One Friday night while I was at home, the phone rang. It was my Boss. "Ron, could you meet me and the Manager of S.K.F. Company at your local restaurant at eight thirty please?" Well, I could not say 'no' and I had a rough idea what it may be about. When I arrived they were both there. I accepted a drink and sat down. "Ron, as you may know, the Company is not producing sufficient parts owing to the problems and down-time of the presses. We need to do something about it so we have had a word with the Company in the U.S.A. and they have offered for someone to go over there to study their production lines etc and we would like you to go over." I sat thinking for a while. I knew it was a heavy responsibility. "You can have a few days break in New York for a rest after you have finished at the Company." said my Boss. "I will do what you've asked, but I must decline the offer of New York as I need to get back because of my sister" I said. He understood. "When you come in on Monday all the arrangements will have been made. Both you and your wife can go to London by rail, stay in an hotel until Tuesday, then you will fly to Detroit and your wife can come back to Birmingham by rail."

Within a few days we were off to London. After settling into our hotel it was nice for us to have a quiet walk around. I had been to London many times for the firm but it was quite an experience for Joan. The next day a taxi took us to the Airport and after a farewell to Joan, she was taken to the station to catch her train home. There was little hanging about at the Airport and I was soon on my way. I occupied myself with a list of things I needed to look at whilst at the American factory. We were told by the pilot that we would arrive late because of strong head winds, and in Detroit they were experiencing heavy snowfalls which would also cause problems. After our long haul, we had difficulty landing owing to the snow storms, but on the third attempt we landed – three and a half hours late!

One of the American engineers whom I had met before in England, had been waiting for me. "Welcome to the U.S.A. Ron. Are you thirsty? Let's have a drink on the way to your hotel – I could do with one!" he exclaimed. It was about 11.45pm U.S.A. time when I arrived at the hotel – all I wanted to do was sleep! "We will pick you up at nine o'clock in the morning. Sleep well." "Thanks Russ, good night" I replied. I knew Russ quite well as I had spent some time with him when he came over to England. He had told me they had arranged for me to use an office next to his when I arrived, so I felt good about that.

The following morning after a quick American style breakfast, I was picked up outside the hotel as promised. It was winter and there was a foot of snow everywhere. Russ met me at the factory and took me to my office where I could do my paperwork on my findings. The owner of the factory came over to me and said, "Welcome to the U.S.A. Ron, I will get Russ to show you around the factory; anything you want just ask; any problem, see me. Russ will show you where my office is. Good luck." I felt a little out of place at first, being in a large American factory, but I had a job to do. After Russ had taken me to every department and introduced me to all the Managers, I went back to my office to take stock of what I had seen and to make a plan as to where I should start. Right at the beginning I decided, when the steel came into the factory, then follow it through its production process and examine every stage.

The first afternoon, I told Russ I had found differences in their steel treatment process compared to ours and also the cutting or cropping stages. When it was almost time to finish for the day I said to Russ that my boss in England had asked me to send by telegram service, every evening, all the information on what I had found. "O.K." said Russ, I will come round at half past eight and we'll go out for a drink." Back at the hotel I had a shower, wrote my reports and posted them at the hotel as they had a telegram service. I then sent for room service and had some food sent up, and waited for Russ. This was to be my routine every evening except at the weekends. Russ I think was glad he had the excuse to come out. I think it was because he had six children and it was his way of having a break! During that first week I discovered several more small things that would help our production. These details I sent off by telegraph each evening so that they could be put to use straight away.

At mid-day on the Friday, Mike the shop floor Manager came over to see me. "Ron, my wife and I want you and Russ to come over to our house for a meal and a drink tonight. I'll pick you up at the hotel at half past eight." I had the feeling it was going to be a bit more than that. The day had been a very fruitful one for me, especially for the number of things I found which we were not doing quite right back at our factory. Like all the other ideas etc I sent the sketches off as soon as I got back to the hotel.

Mike picked us up as promised, and he told me that near to his home was a large lake which was frozen at that time. As we went past I was surprised to see quite a few little huts on the ice, with lights in them. Mike explained that in each one was one of his neighbours and they were fishing through a hole in the ice! "They must be crazy" I said. We went up a drive to his house where his garage doors opened automatically and all the lights came on. I had a very pleasant welcome from his wife and children and about half an hour later we were sitting down to a lovely steak meal, followed by coffee. "Can you play Pool Ron?" Mike asked. "No" I replied, "but I have played Snooker a few times." "Good, follow me" he said, and led me down into his basement. Inside were about eight of the engineers I had been working alongside. They'd obviously had this planned. There was a Pool table and a bar in the corner. "What do you drink Ron?" asked Mike. "I'd like a Gin and Orange please." "No problem" and his wife handed me a large glass of Gin with pure orange juice, which was filled up twice more during the evening. I believe it was about 2.15am when I was finally driven back to the hotel! I don't remember much about the drive back, so Saturday morning I did not bother about breakfast, and decided to go for a walk to clear my head.

Across the main road was a foot bridge leading to a large shopping centre where there was everything you could want – even guns were on open display. I had my lunch at a self-service bar where you could help yourself to as much as you wanted at a fixed price. After that I decided to go back to the hotel and rest a while. At about half past three, while I was watching television, the phone in the room rang. It was the Representative from the factory. He lived over the border in Canada about forty miles away. "Ron, how would you like to come over to our place for the evening? I can pick you up at six thirty, and I'll invite a couple of my neighbours over too. I'll get you back for midnight." I could not very well refuse, and it sounded good, so I said, "O.K. thanks, I will wait here for you." I could at least say I had been to Canada, even if it was only for a few hours!

Richard had emigrated from England to Canada twelve years previously. His wife Chris was from London, and according to Richard, was longing to go back to England. This was quite evident when I met her as when he introduced me to her it was as though I was some long lost friend showing up! She would only talk about England. "What's it like now over there, Ron?" she asked. "Much better than just after the war" I replied. "Have you ever tried eating those rotten American sausages? They really are awful!" she told me. "No, I haven't tried one yet" I said. We had a very pleasant evening, mainly talking about England. Their neighbours had never met another English person it seemed, by the questions they asked. The evening went very quickly and as Richard knew I'd previously had a very late night, at eleven o'clock he was ready to take me back. We had all enjoyed the evening and we wished each other well and I thanked his wife. It was a good straight road and we by-passed Detroit, arriving at the hotel just after midnight. "Have a good rest tomorrow" Richard said, and wished me good night and set off home.

I slept like a log that night and took it easy all Sunday. Russ picked me up in the evening and took me for a drive along the main highway. "Do you fancy a hot-dog?" asked Russ. "Yes, why not" I said, but I immediately thought of Richard's wife and what she had said about American sausages. We went to a hot-dog stall about a mile up the road. A Mexican-looking chap with a big bushy moustache served us. "Two medium hot-dogs, Bud" said Russ, "with plenty of chilli on." The man picked up two large bread rolls, already slit open, and stuck in a huge hot sausage about nine inches long, then poured the hot chilli sauce all along the sausage. They were handed to us on a throw-away plate. "Well Russ, I have been dying to try one of these" I said. The first thing was to open my mouth wide enough. I made the mistake of not holding the roll tightly enough and biting it near the end. The bloody sausage shot straight out with the slimy chilli on it and slid along the table. Russ started to choke on his when he saw what had happened! I ended up holding the sausage in one hand and the bread roll in the other, nibbling at them in turn. Richard's wife was right, the skins on the sausages were like rubber. I was being watched by another American chap, a puzzled look on his face as he saw me eating like that! Half way through it I'd had enough and gave up. "Fancy going for a beer?" Russ asked. "A good idea" I said with relief. "I'll take you to a bar where there are 'Go-Go' girls" he said. "What the bloody hell are 'Go-Go' girls?" I asked. "You'll see" was the reply.

We drove to a bar just down the road; quite a nice looking place. We sat down and a girl waiter came up behind me to get our order. When I turned to speak to her

I saw she was bloody topless!! When I looked round, all the waiters were girls and all were topless and when they were serving, they did not seem to bother at all!

"Well, Russ, I think I have seen everything now!" I exclaimed, "but it's eleven o'clock and I have a lot more work to do tomorrow." "O.K. it's about time we went" he said. When he dropped me off at the hotel, I said, "Thank you Russ for all you've done for me – see you tomorrow."

There was a lot I had planned to do on the Monday, so I was very busy and the day went quickly. At about four thirty I was called to the phone in the main office. It was my Boss in England. "How are you Ron?" he said. "We have looked at some of the ideas you have sent and we are getting them drawn up and detailed. They are obviously going to be better." "I have some more to send you, particularly on the feeding devices" I told him. "Very good, Ron; see you in ten days time. Good luck." That message bucked me up and I felt I was not wasting my time.

As I was leaving for the hotel, the owner of the factory stopped me. "I'm going to pick you up at eight o'clock tomorrow evening, along with Russ, to take you both out for a meal, if you have no other arrangements." "No, I haven't," I said, "we will look forward to that –

thank you." I did my usual routine when I got to the hotel – a good clean up, get my reports off, have a bite to eat, and out with Russ, my faithful friend. However, I insisted we had an early night. Whilst waiting for him I sent for room service, i.e. a bottle of whiskey and a chicken sandwich.

The following day, Tuesday, I went to the tool-room Manager for some information. I had met Tommy the week before; a really good engineer with lots of practical experience. I had found out that there was a special machine-building shop where they also built special purpose machinery under licence for another factory. At that time they were building an automatic Cold-Heading machine (only an engineer would know what that is) and it was the biggest in the world. I had been invited the next day to see it tried out for the first time.

"Tom" I asked, "why on earth do you take on such enormous tasks when there is a possibility they may not work?" "Well, Ron, engineering must advance" he said. "If we have an idea that might be possible, we have a go at it, getting over all the problems on the way." "That reminds me of a quotation by Albert Einstein that I read – he said, 'It's not that I am intelligent – I just stick with the problem until it is done'" I told him. Tom thought that was typical of what they were doing.

I continued with more problem searching but left a bit earlier as I was going out later with the Boss and Russ. The Boss was German by birth and had come to the U.S.A. when a young man. He had set up business near Detroit in the motor manufacturing area, to produce car components. Dead on eight o'clock he collected Russ and me and took us to a rather up-market restaurant. After he had bought us a drink he asked, "Do you both like steak?" "We certainly do" we replied. So three large steak meals were ordered, the likes of which I had never seen! They were brought in on a plate of their own with all the vegetables on a separate tray. We could not have a continuous conversation with meals of this size, but the conversation was mainly about travelling the world because the Boss had done so much. It was interesting having a conversation with such a successful man who was an engineer in his own right. After the coffee, he said to me, "Ron, if you ever decide to live in the States, there's a job here for you." I think that summed it up that he thought I was O.K. It made me feel contented. He was obviously not a man to hang about so we were soon off, and after dropping me off at the hotel, he said "I will see you again before you leave on Saturday. Good night." I thanked him for the lovely evening, went to my room and after a quick swill I fell on the bed and slept like a log.

On the Wednesday morning I spent most of my time writing reports and making sketches to be sent back to England that evening. In the afternoon I was invited to the Boss's office along with a number of his top engineers to discuss those first trials of the new machine. I was certainly learning more about how the firm worked. After about an hour we all moved into the machine-building department. I was amazed at its size. We had one of those in our factory in England, but nothing on that scale. The engineers proceeded to check everything over – the electrics, safety equipment etc. This took about an hour, then the Boss gave the O.K. to give it a short trial. After a while the power was switched off and the components it had produced were examined. They all went back to the office for further discussions but I stayed to have a closer look at the machine before going back to my office. "I was amazed" I told Russ, who had not yet seen it.

I told Russ not to bother to pick me up that night as I just wanted to have a quiet evening and it would give him a break as he had been so good to me. I think he wanted a break too. After I had settled down in the hotel, I sent for a pot of tea and some chicken sandwiches then watched the television.

On Thursday I went back over everything I had seen before, to make sure I hadn't missed anything. I did find a few more useful items we could improve on, but I decided not to send anything by telegraph as I would be on my way home on the Saturday. Tommy, the tool-room Manager, invited me to his house for a meal and to meet his family. I think I must have put on half a stone since I had arrived in the U.S.A! It was a pleasant evening with his family. Everyone had been so kind and friendly whilst I was there – people I would never see again, but would always remember when I got home.

I did a bit more work on Friday morning and in the afternoon the Boss phoned me and asked me to pop in his office. He gave me a glass of whiskey and wished me all the best and a safe journey home. I tidied up the office I had been using and collected all my belongings then went around the whole factory to say good-bye to all those I had met, and thanked them all for their very generous help. I popped in to see Tommy and on the wall by his desk he had written the quote by Albert Einstein I had told him about. 'It's not that I am intelligent – I just stick with the problem until it is done.' "That will remind me of your visit, Ron" he said, and that was the last I saw of him.

Russ came over to the hotel later that evening. He came up to my room and we sat there chatting and finishing off the whiskey I had, and arranging the details for getting to the Airport as my plane was to leave at ten thirty the next morning. "I'll pick you up at nine o'clock, Ron. That will give plenty of time. Good night."

I did not sleep very well that night, wondering if I had done enough investigation and if I had missed anything out which I had been asked to look at – but it was too late now!

After a good breakfast, Russ arrived as usual bang on time. It was a great shame that I may never see him again after that day. At the Airport we stood talking for a while before I had the O.K. to board the plane. Once again I thanked him and said good-bye. I was surprised that no-one else was aboard, so I picked a seat near the escape door so I could stretch my legs out. The steward told me the main number of passengers would be picked up at Boston. After the plane took off, I fell fast asleep for the whole journey and when I did wake up I looked through the window and I could see green fields below – I was over England! It seemed strange – one minute I was in Detroit and the next I was in England – everything was going too quickly. Before I picked up a taxi to take me to Euston Station, I phoned Joan to arrange for my son to pick me up in Birmingham. Once again, I fell asleep on the train.

I could not believe how tired I must have been to sleep so much. I remembered little about the journey from Boston to Birmingham! Almost as soon as I got off the train, I spotted my son looking out for me. In less than half an hour I was back with Joan. I had only been away for two and a half weeks, but I felt so good to be back with her and my children.

I had a phone call from my Boss suggesting I took a couple of days off to rest and get used to the time difference. This I did, though during the weekend my first priority was to see my sister who was now very ill with cancer. I found she was keeping a brave face, although she was suffering, but there was very little I could do or say to help her.

However, back at work I needed to implement the changes as most of these would be done through the Tool-room of which I was in charge. I was pleased to find that things had not stood still whilst I was away and lots of the modifications had already been implemented. The Boss walked round with me and said, "The two main presses have increased their production rate already and with less down-time." "It's been worth while then" I remarked, "but there are a lot more modifications to do yet."

"Yes, we have to get moving as soon as possible" he replied.

CHAPTER NINETEEN

At home we had more concern for my sister as her illness had become very serious towards the end of the year, and she died just before Christmas – a very sad time for us all.

Our children were growing up fast. My elder son, David, was now married and my other son, Robert, was studying hard and was fast becoming skilful in art. My daughter, Valerie, was also studying and all three seemed at this stage to be showing intellect and a respectful attitude.

Back at work the pressure was still on and although the firm was producing well, the demand for different components to be manufactured by the new process was causing ever more problems with further development.

One Monday morning, not long after I had arrived at work, my other sister phoned to tell me my father had passed away early that morning. He was nearly eighty two years old and never complained of his problems. Knowing the history of the man I was thankful he had died peacefully and suddenly. My mother was now on her own but as usual was coping well under the circumstances – but then she always did. My parents had been married for sixty two years.

Over the last few years I had been having minor health problems. The pressure of work never relented. I was looking after the Tool-room and the Development Department and was then asked to take over as Safety Officer too. I was then fifty five. One weekend I felt quite ill and during the early hours of Monday I had a heart attack which kept me off work for five weeks. I knew I could not carry on in the same way so I gave up the post of Safety Officer, and delegated more work to the Charge-hand. I also found the continual noise of the heavy presses thumping away all day in the Production Department was getting to me, as in the course of my work I had to oversee the results of any changes there and sort out any problems in the development stages that often occurred.

I became very irritable at times at home. I had spent all my life in engineering and I knew that it had to end. Joan, just like my mother, showed her extreme understanding of the situation, which helped me a great deal. The Boss had obviously noticed I was taking less interest in everything and a couple of months before I was sixty one years of age, I asked to see him. "I've worked for the firm for twenty nine years now" I said, "and I don't wish to stay until I'm sixty five because of my health, so I would be grateful if you would consider making me redundant."

"I cannot do that" was his reply. "But my health is suffering" I reminded him. He made no comment other than to say "But you're not redundant, so I cannot do it."

"O.K. then, I will have to consider the situation myself" I said, and walked out of his office.

When I arrived home I had a long conversation with Joan. She was very concerned but very understanding, and I tried to assure her things would be O.K. By January I had made up my mind. I was not going to make my health any worse for the sake of money, and on the 3rd of February I went to see my Boss, and told him that I wished to give a weeks notice and leave on my sixty first birthday. There were a few moments of silence then he said, "I can't give you any redundancy money as you are ending your employment with us yourself." "I'm not expecting any redundancy money, though I thought you may give me some sort of severance pay" I said. "I'm not sure I can do that either" he replied. Anyway I was not going to change my mind or beg for money; I had already made up my mind about that. I had never done that before and I was not about to start. I had never been money-motivated and had made sure a few years before, that I would pay off my mortgage in case of a situation like this. "I'm sorry you are leaving us, but Good Luck to you" the Boss said, and that was that. I left the following Friday but before I went, I popped into the Boss's office. I wished him luck and shook hands with him. There was no way I was leaving with ill feelings or bearing a grudge – that would not have been any good at all. I walked out and never went back to those works again.

Whatever had happened over the years, I had learned a great deal about myself, and my knowledge of engineering had given me a lot of confidence. I had also learned that there was a sinister side of industry, though most of the time I was too pre-occupied to give it any thought. Other companies would try to get technical information about production or development in a very underhand way. I was in a position to acquire and use all the drawings regarding our production methods and I was once contacted by a man I had met at a very large Birmingham engineering works. He suggested a certain cash payment by his company for copies of these carefully controlled drawings. I firmly told him he was asking something I would not do and I would never be disloyal to my company. His firm is no longer in existence, and neither is he.

I was also responsible for the manufacture of all production tools of which there were a great many, so a good amount of the work had to be contracted out to other tool making firms. This amounted to thousands of pound per month. One day I had a phone call from the Receptionist. "There's a man here who is asking to see you, Ron. He's a Rep. from another tool making firm." I went down to Reception and was greeted by a very smart man. "Hello Ron" he said, as though he'd known me for years – but I had never met him before. It was close to lunch time and he said "Would you like to come to the local pub and I will buy you a meal and we can discuss things over a drink." Well, I never did accept free meals from Reps unless I knew them well. "No thanks, I have my meal ordered in the canteen" I said. "O.K. then, let me show you our catalogue over in the car" he replied. When outside, he told me he knew that I sent out lots of contracts for tool manufacture to small tool-making firms. He also remarked that he knew it was a considerable amount. "If you give our firm all these contracts, I will personally see to it that you will get a new car after the first three months" he said. Although I had previously been told about this sort of dealing, I did not think it would happen to me! I immediately sent him packing and warned him not to come to the factory again. But whatever my feelings were I had made up my mind I would not get involved in such dealings, and I'm glad I never did. My Boss had told me that our Accountant had received bills from firms unknown to us and if not checked out properly, cheques could be signed and sent out. Luckily our Accountant was wise to this and was able to keep his eye on it.

One month after I had retired I received a cheque for £6,500 from the Accountant with little explanation what it was for, but I was glad to accept it. Another two months after that I met up with a chap who had worked for me in the Tool-room. "Hello Ron, how are you getting on?" he asked. "I feel much better in health and I'm making a few quid on the side with the aid of my old contacts" I replied. "Have you heard about the factory?" he enquired. "No, what's that?" I said. "A couple of months after you left they sold the factory to another company" he told me. "Well, unless they have plenty of experience of that method of production they will never last" I predicted. "They'll need men with years of knowledge and practical experience." Some time later I discovered that my prediction was right, as the firm that had taken the business over had given up and closed down. I was disappointed as a lot of hard work for a lot of people for many years had gone into it.

About six months after I had left work, after many tests, it was discovered I had Paget's disease of the spine and during the scans it was also found I was developing Prostate problems. Also about that time, my brother Jim who had been suffering with ill health, passed away at home. He was sixty three.

My family and my health were now my priority. My elder son David and his wife Yvonne had two children, a son named Martyn and a daughter, Tina – so Joan and I were Grand-parents! Valerie, my daughter, was married to Chris who was a mechanic and shop manager. Robert, my younger son, was courting Jenny who he had met at college – a well-spoken and educated girl. I had met her father a few times in the course of my Safety Officer training. He did a lot of lecturing on the subject as he was Chairman of RoSPA.

I was getting involved in all sorts of jobs to earn some extra cash – repairing clocks, watches, long-case clocks, furniture, French-polishing etc, in fact anything that came along. But as I was getting older, time was taking its toll. My mother had died at the age of ninety one. Her life could tell a real story. She was a very bright woman, constantly reading all her life. She always had to be doing something – a bit of a workaholic, and a really good person who loved her family.

My health was deteriorating and I was in constant discomfort with Angina pains. Then at the age of sixty eight I had to have a triple by-pass operation. With Joan's help and support, I got over it well and felt fitter than I had been for years!

Now at the age of eighty three, as I look back over the years I can only say I am a lucky man. I have escaped the ravages of war and survived the illnesses I have had, and most of all having the good fortune to meet Joan, my very patient and uncomplaining wife. I know at times I have been a difficult person to live with, and Joan herself had had problems of mobility after two hip replacements.

When I came out of the Army and had been back at work a couple of years, my engineering opportunities seemed to get better and better. I adopted a practical approach to most problems which saw me through and with the eventual position I held, it had given me the chance to visit several engineering factories and meet many good engineers. There were companies such as Ferranti of Edinburgh, Bellis and Morecombe of Birmingham, Lockheed, Joseph Lucas, High Duty Alloys and Garringtons of Redditch, SKF of Luton and Braun Engineering Co. of Detroit U.S.A. and many more. I believe the road to a successful life is a contented mind – sometimes very difficult to achieve. If you have that, I think not a great deal more is required.

CHAPTER TWENTY

Our children have been very good and are all hard-working. David, our eldest, has now been married for thirty four years, and although he has swapped jobs fairly regularly he continues to work hard for his family, but more important, he is a very generous person.

Valerie, our daughter, is a loyal and hard worker. She has worked in factory laboratories, has been the local school secretary and now, after a lot of studying has achieved a First Class Honours Degree and is now an Occupational Therapist. Her husband, Chris, and her two boys are very proud of her, as is all the family.

Our younger son, Robert, has worked very hard, both academically and physically. His life has not been easy, but he has agreed for me to tell his story – a difficult one to tell, but important because of the effect it has had on our family and also because it may help others in similar circumstances. It is necessary for me to explain all this for what we were to find out a few years later, and why it was so difficult for me to take in and understand.

Robert was born on the 17th December 1952. As he grew up, as a young boy he seemed to be very quiet and even a bit withdrawn at times, but he was soon to grow out of that when he started school. There were obvious signs to us that he was quite intelligent and would do well, so Joan and I were not worried for his future. At the age of eleven, to our surprise, he failed the Eleven Plus exam. Robert was an individual and had his own way of working things out and what he did, he did well. Soon after, he went to Secondary School – different teachers and different methods of teaching. He soon started to show exactly what he was capable of and proved he liked things done properly with no half-measures.

He soon palled up with a boy who lived in the village; a very bright lad who in later life did exceptionally well. Together they joined the local Air Training Corps.

They seemed to develop a strong bond as both seemed to have an adventurous spirit. During one school holiday they decided to hitch-hike to the Norfolk area where there were several British and American Military Airfields. They planned to ask at the airfields if there were any jobs they could do to help and at the same time learn something of the running of the Air Force and find out more about military aircraft. At one American Airfield they were welcomed in and even given their own sleeping quarters. After helping out with chores they would sometimes be taken on flights and served coffee to the crew. The boys seemed to get on well with everyone and enjoyed the experience and adventure. When it was time to return home, they again hitch-hiked all the way back. All this was done on their own initiative, and their bold natures were to be of help in later life.

At sixteen, Robert's artistic skills had been recognised and when he left school he was given a job in a drawing and design office. At that time, I had apprentices in my department at work and I knew the college training negotiator well. He told me that he considered Robert to be too good for the job he had, and thought he should go to college to further his skills. Robert still at times seemed to be rather quiet and a bit stressed, but with all he was doing, I wasn't worried. He went to college as advised, and it was there he met Jenny who was later to become his wife. After two years of hard study, his tutor suggested he should go to University as he had advanced to a point where college could no longer help him. He acquired the necessary qualifications for University and after many months of study, gained a First Class Honours Degree in Graphic Illustration.

During his time at University I again at odd times, had noticed visual signs of stress as though something else was bothering him, but as we knew how hard he was working, we dismissed it.

After a while, Robert and Jenny decided to get married, and at the reception I asked Robert what his plans were, as he never said much about his future. Without hesitation he said "We are going to travel before we are too old to do so, and see a bit of life abroad. First we are going to Australia." This came as a big surprise to us, although we were aware that they both loved adventure – so we wished them well.

Robert was not a big young man, but he was very fit. His wife was a very bright, intelligent and resilient girl, and they both knew exactly what they were doing and what they wanted. Soon after the wedding, they put the plans together and flew to Singapore where they stayed for six weeks. During that time they found that a Russian Liner was sailing to Australia and they arranged their passage. Whilst on the Liner, Robert became ill and on arrival in Australia saw a doctor who diagnosed Hepatitis. He advised them to return home, but Robert was determined to stay and accomplish what he had set out to do. We only found out about his illness some months later, from someone who had met them in Australia – it was typical of Robert to say nothing, to save us worrying!

After he had recovered, they purchased a large old American car which would be able to carry all the items needed for a mining expedition, such as a metal detector and digging and panning tools. Then they contacted the local Planning Department to acquire a mining licence as is required in Australia. Having stocked up with provisions, they set off into the Outback and gold mining areas and started their search. When they ran out of provisions, they would find the nearest town and both get a job doing anything to earn enough cash to re-stock and return to the Outback.

We had many letters and photos from them although it was quite a long time later that we learned about all their Australian adventures. However, it was obvious they were doing exactly what they had planned to do, and seemed happy. One day when they were many miles from any town, Robert had discovered a dried-up river bed on his map which showed an early mining area. He had left Jenny in the tent to cook up some food. After he had been mining for a few hours, he returned only to find Jenny had collapsed with dehydration. He quickly packed up everything and took her to a place many miles away where they found a volunteer ambulance crew. Unfortunately the driver was drunk in the local bar, but eventually another man offered to drive Jenny to hospital some one hundred and fifty miles away, with Robert following in his old car. Luckily Jenny soon recovered, and they returned to the Outback and continued with their gold mining.

They had been away for about twelve months, and had almost circumnavigated Australia. They then started out again in the southern part and continued north through Alice Springs where they stayed for a while and lived with the local inhabitants, before finally arriving in the northern area eighteen months later. After a few weeks rest, they flew home.

Back in England, Robert took a teaching post at a college in Derby and after some time there an offer came for him to go to Papua New Guinea on a three year teaching contract. In the meantime they had purchased an old stone-built cottage in Herefordshire, which had been a school house. After having it fully renovated they moved in and soon after, Jenny gave birth to their daughter Elizabeth. The cottage was ideal and in a lovely spot. Whilst waiting for all the arrangements to be finalised for the job in Papua, Robert was still teaching and travelling a great deal in England, and I frequently noticed the look of stress and anxiety in his face, and would ask if everything was O.K. though I never seemed to get a convincing answer.

Eventually they set off for Papua New Guinea and left Joan and me to look after their affairs here, and the cottage which we frequently used for our holiday breaks. We were quite worried about them travelling in that country, but knew from past experience that they wouldn't tell us of any illness or mishap until well after it had passed. But both our other children were the same – I suppose it was to try and stop us from worrying!

Soon they started to send letters and photos, and I can only say that the things they did whilst over there can only be described as risky and daring, and many other adventurous people would be envious of what they did! During his teaching breaks, they would venture deep into the jungle or go down crocodile-infested rivers in a dug-out canoe with two natives. Jenny took photos of Robert teasing a large crocodile with a stick as it tried to get out of the river and up a steep bank! On another of these breaks, Robert wanted to film a particular tribe who were known to have been head hunters some years earlier, and taking their young daughter with them, they again went up the river in a dug-out canoe. With the aid of one of his pupils, who knew the area, they eventually found the natives' encampment. Permission from the tribe had to be acquired before they were allowed into the camp, and when this was given they lived with the tribe for a few days, sleeping among them in their stilted huts along the riverbank.

Jenny at the time was pregnant, and later gave birth to their son Andrew, and they decided to also give him the Papua name of 'Yama' which means 'the pretty one'! His birth had taken place, we understand, in the Doctor's surgery. We also found out later that during their time over there, Robert had had pneumonia and their daughter had contracted malaria. Thankfully they both fully recovered.

After completing the three years over there, the family settled down in Herefordshire, living in the converted school house. Robert continued teaching and much travelling to various colleges. Once again I noticed how stressed he seemed to be, but I did not question it as I thought it was all due to the travelling and getting home late.

After living there for a few years they found a disused farm property with twelve acres of land. The buildings needed to be partly rebuilt and completely renovated. They decided to purchase this property, and while living in an old mobile home, they set about the rebuild and renovation which I considered a mammoth task for them. The farm was four miles from the nearest village but they were not deterred by this, and worked as hard as ever. Many a weekend I would go over myself and give a hand. Even so, it took a long time to complete. It was no surprise to me to realise that Robert was suffering under the strain of so much work, but he definitely seemed to have other things on his mind. Occasionally I would ask Jenny if all was O.K.

"Yes, he's alright" would always be the answer.

After about ten years at the farm, a place they never farmed themselves, but rented out the fields to local farmers for their sheep to graze, it eventually was getting too much for them what with long distance travelling and the costly up-keep of the place. Jenny was travelling to Hereford Hospital for her nursing job and Robert sometimes had to travel as far as York. Finally they decided to sell up, and they bought an old Victorian house in the city of Hereford, which straight away eased their travelling time and expenditure. The house had been used as a children's home and had six bedrooms, but it needed complete renovation. Once again it was to be no half measures for Robert – it all had to be done properly. There was a very large back garden which they transformed to perfection.

Their daughter, Elizabeth, had grown up into a fine, bright and intelligent girl who was very talented in art, and had won a place in the Royal College of Art in London. Their son, Andrew, was becoming a very responsible young man who was doing very well at college, so there were no worries with the children. However, at this time, I was convinced something was wrong, though I could not put my finger on it. Once again I asked Jenny, "Is Robert alright?" and the same answer would come, "Yes, he's fine." But I was not convinced. I thought perhaps there was something wrong with their marriage, though did not ask that question. I had noticed that Robert had let his hair grow longer, which was unusual for him. He was also spending a lot of time in his garden. It looked so lovely that he did an oil painting of it. He was now forty nine years old, and still worked as hard and precisely as ever.

A few weeks later, Joan and I went over on a Sunday to spend the day with them. When we arrived Robert was not in the house. "Where's Robert?" I asked Jenny. "Oh, he's in the garden." I went out to find him and as I walked down the garden I spotted him – he was rubbing his head hard, as if in complete frustration and anxiety, but immediately he saw me he took on a normal posture. "Are you alright, Robert?" I asked. "Yes, I'm fine" he replied, though it was obvious to me he was not. When I went back into the house, I again asked Jenny, "Is Robert alright?" "Yes, he's O.K." was the answer once more. But I could tell she was covering something up. Another thing I had noticed was that Robert had dyed his hair a light brown, which seemed very unusual for him. I discussed all this with Joan on the way home, but I had no positive answer from her, though it was obvious she had noticed all these things too, and was concerned.

About two weeks later, on a Saturday morning, I was having a lie-in. Joan had been up for some time, when she came into the bedroom and sat on the side of the bed and said, "I have something to tell you." For Joan to do this it was obviously going to be something very serious. "Robert had been suffering with a gender problem for some time, and he is going to have to change his sex." I was speechless, and yet I seemed to have half known it all the time, but could not readily accept what I was thinking. It was now very clear what had been on his mind for such a very long time.

Over the next few weeks, I learned that Robert, ever since he was a young man, had this feeling of uncertainty about himself, though I never knew. He had obviously gone through years of worry and kept it to himself. When he met Jenny, he had told her of this problem before they were married, but she stood by him. We discovered that this gender problem can come about in the early stages of pregnancy, and there's nothing one can do about it. When I learned about Robert's predicament I felt guilty and ashamed that I had not noticed anything, and he'd had to carry the burden on his own for so many years.

It was unknown to me at the time, that he had been seeing specialists. I can now fully understand why he seemed to be suffering from something. But the amount of hard physical work he was putting into his properties, and his adventures abroad, suggested nothing of his conflict. It was now obvious he had reached a stage in his river of life when he had to make up his mind to cross that bridge from which there was no return, and become a woman. It was now that I felt my guilt for not seeing this, and I felt I should have shown more caring at times instead of concentrating on my own problems and interests.

Robert had now made up his mind and supported by Jenny, he eventually went through with the change, and as always with him, there would be no half measures – it had to be done properly. Some men, during their lives just want to look like a woman for various reasons – maybe for entertainment or just to be noticed, but not for Robert. It seemed as though nature had taken a wrong turning before he was born over which no one had any control. Joan and I have read of many experiences of families who have had to try and understand this problem and come to terms with it, as we have had to ourselves.

Fortunately so many people have understood and supported him. Our family, his wife and two children have shown him the love and understanding he needed. His wife's relatives have demonstrated their support and also his many trusted friends and people he has worked with. His sister Valerie and her husband Chris, had known some time before I had, and both have been solid in their caring and understanding towards him and his family.

After Robert had completed all the necessary operations, he and his wife did the correct thing, as they always do, and on the 9th of January 2006 they became civil partners after going through a legal procedure which ended their marriage. They are officially recognised as civil partners by law, and he is no longer known as Robert, but Bobby. It has been quite difficult for us, his parents, to get out of the habit of saying 'Robert' and to refer to 'him' as 'her.'

Bobby now appears to be much more relaxed and to have found peace of mind. Jenny too seems contented and their children are very supportive. Everything has been done with trust, love and understanding.

David, our eldest, has found it difficult to accept and still is reluctant to meet Bobby, though we're sure he will eventually. We have learned it is commonplace for a brother to have difficulty in taking the change on board. Perhaps that is another twist of nature.

We are aware that there are those who may scoff and ridicule, but they are misguided and have no understanding of such genuine problems.

This part of my story has been written with the full consent and support of Bobby and the family in the hope that others may be helped.

CHAPTER TWENTY ONE

If I now look back very briefly over my past life, I would probably say yes, there are things I would do differently, only as much as to try and do certain things better. I would have liked to have done more for Joan and my children, but I would not have wanted to be more ambitious. The essence of a good life is a contended mind which at odd times I lost through things I did not understand.

I remember vividly when I was ten years old; I was in the playground at school and I was teasing a rather timid boy because of his thick glasses. The Head Master saw this and took me into his office. Normally it would have been a good walloping with three good strokes of the cane. As I was a small boy for my age, he stood me on a stool facing the black-board on which he proceeded to write this quotation.

'Life is just like froth and bubble
But two things stand like stone
Kindness in another's trouble
And courage in your own'

"Now stand there and read it over and over again until you cannot forget it" he said. Well, I did as I was told until I fully understood its meaning, and I have never forgotten it. I told my mother what had been done and why. I knew my mother would appreciate that kind of approach – it's exactly the kind of thing she would have done in similar circumstances. I know at times I was a little sod at home, but I never had a walloping from either of my parents; it was always a good stiff talking to. I suppose I have not always lived up to those words during my life, but many times when I have been angry, they have made me stop to think if I was acting correctly.

At this stage of my story, I must ask myself what I am and if my life's experiences have altered me in any way. I know I have had to side-slip my own story to tell of my middle child, but he – or I should say she – had the courage to eventually face up to the life change, and both Bobby and Jenny wanted me to tell that story as they hoped it would help others in similar situations. Personally I don't think I have changed at all, and there's the old saying 'a leopard never changes his spots.'

I think the first ten years of my life, during the hardship days for my parents, fashioned my character and I believe in the later years I was just learning the real facts of life – most of those being my war experiences which were and are, the most vivid. As with many people, the older I became, the wiser I became. Sadly, things I see now make me feel somewhat disappointed, especially when I think of the many who gave their lives for their countries and what they believed in. In some ways they have been let down and I often wonder what they would say if they could see the world as it is now.

I have been back to France a few times and always make a point of going to the war graves. The first time I went back I visited the Military Cemetery at Hermonville, an area I knew well, and as I walked around I remembered some of the names of the men I'd known, one of whom I'd met at the camp in Shrewsbury. The War Graves Commission do a wonderful job with the care and maintenance of the cemeteries, nothing out of place, and we ex-servicemen and the families of the deceased are so touched and thankful for their care. But in my thoughts I see a different picture. I see, as many others who have witnessed the horrors of war, the traumatic and painful manner in which those servicemen died and it seems to be hidden in those very serene places.

There are many memorial monuments in this country and elsewhere, where services and parades are held to honour and remember those who died in conflicts, and it is only right we should do so. The British Armed Forces have fought many great battles all over the world over many years, but probably none so well considered and brilliantly planned as the deception regarding the D-Day landings on the Normandy beaches on the 6th June 1944, which carried such great risks for its success, so much so that even a man like Joseph Stalin once said of it:

'The history of war does not know of an undertaking comparable to it for breadth of conception, grandeur of scale and mastery of execution.'

Yet it saddens me we do not have an annual flag-day for it. The main disappointment for me though, is what we have allowed to happen in our country since the war. We have allowed a continuing deterioration of morality throughout our nation, and over the past forty years a drug culture has spiralled out of control, which in turn has caused so much trauma and misery for those who have been caught up in it, something which I believe could have been halted all those years ago. I feel deeply that it is not what all those people died for and unfortunately they cannot voice their opinion.

It also dismays me that there are many people who have been allowed to live in this country who have no desire to abide by our customs. Some even try to force their beliefs on others, and are prepared to commit murder in the name of religion. Unfortunately the Civil Rights Movement at times seem to have created an imbalance of law between the perpetrator and the victim. Is this what those servicemen and women died for? I think not, and I'm sure many people think the same. I am as patriotic as my parents and try to remember what this country has always stood for, and the armies that have defended it. As Sir Winston Churchill said:

'A nation that forgets its past, soon loses its identity.'

It has been interesting for me to look back on my life for this story, and it has not always been easy to remember everything, but I have not tried to enhance the facts. I know I have not been perfect, but have tried to learn from the example of others. To my family I owe so much for their kindness and care. In my old age, being an impatient person, I do get a bit grumpy at times, not being able to do things that I have always taken for granted. I have never shunned hard work and have difficulty in coming to terms with not being able to do as much as in the past. But I suppose I had better finish my story before I'm thought of as a moaning old devil! I just hope that anyone reading my story may appreciate it and be grateful for what they have.

I have now been married to Joan for fifty nine years and I know it has been me who at times has rocked the boat and upset Joan with my lack of patience. But Joan, being the opposite, has probably created the right balance with all that has happened over the years. I know full well I am a very lucky person, but I believe in the saying:

'If you want a rainbow in your life, you have to put up with a little rain.'

And now perhaps I will be even more lucky, and live long enough to reach that illusive sixty years of marriage which has proved so difficult for so many.